The lightning had struck the bedroom area and the reason the fire burned so intensely was because the mattress and bedding must have instantly ignited. If the dog had not coaxed him outside, he most likely would have died in that bed.

When he told his story to his neighbor, the man was perplexed. "The dog you describe sounds like Sandy," the man said, slowly shaking his head. "She was a setter but with that very unusual marking of a white chest and neck. . . ."

"That must be her, all right. My God, where is she? I think I have to thank her for my life!" Talbert exclaimed.

The neighbor didn't say anything for several moments. He stared at Talbert and then slumped in his chair. His voice was hardly audible as he whispered, "That won't be possible, Frank. She died more than two months ago."

ANIMAL IMMORTALITY

A Startling Revelation About Pets and Their Afterlife

Bill D. Schul

FAWCETT GOLD MEDAL · NEW YORK

A Fawcett Gold Medal Book
Published by Ballantine Books
Copyright © 1991 by Bill D. Schul

All rights reserved under International and Pan-American Copyright Conventions. Published in the United States by Ballantine Books, a division of Random House, Inc., New York, and simultaneously in Canada by Random House of Canada Limited, Toronto.

Library of Congress Catalog Card Number: 90-1327

ISBN 0-449-14748-7

This edition published by arrangement with Carroll & Graf Publishers, Inc.

Manufactured in the United States of America

First Ballantine Books Edition: February 1992

Grid photo © Michael Tchererk/The Image Bank
Cat Photo © Cara Moore/The Image Bank

CONTENTS

CHAPTER ONE

Awareness of Death

Do animals have souls? Does something of the creature remain after death? What claim, if any, can it make on immortality?

There is a general assumption in our culture that only humans are blessed with souls and immortal life, that once an animal's brief span is spent upon the earth, it is gone forever except as its memory lingers on in the hearts of those who loved it.

Is this assumption true? Upon what facts is it based? What is the evidence to the contrary?

The reader is invited to explore these and many other questions pertaining to animal survival of bodily death, and in the pages which follow the greatest adventure of all will be undertaken: the journey to the world beyond this one. Is it really unknown? Does existing knowledge reveal that we share this odyssey with our fellow creatures? If animals survive death, what is their destiny? What is the purpose behind their lives, death, and going on to other states?

These are cosmic questions, ones entertained by man about himself since the beginning of time. Inasmuch as they remain, permeating every aspect of our lives, they continue to intrigue and haunt us. Is this curiosity and apprehension of death limited to the human species? Although we readily accept animal instinct for survival as nature's way of protecting life upon this planet, we have not extended a knowledge of death to creatures other than ourselves.

We concede that humans share the instinct for survival, but we have assumed that our love of life and fear of death as the annihilation of ourselves is limited to our species alone. We understand that life is sweet but all too brief, and its pleasures are haunted by the spectre of death waiting in the wings to drop the curtain—perhaps without notice on ourselves and those we love. We witness the passage of time, the unrelentless erosion of age, and ponder the meaning of it all.

We harbor the thought that only we cling to life as a precious commodity. As a rule, we do not entertain the idea that other animals experience anxiety or fear of death. We imagine that, since they do not comprehend that life will end, death has no meaning to them.

While we cannot discuss this issue with animals, there are other ways we can reexamine the question. Investigation of animal behavior reveals some rather thought-provoking observations of animal response to and anticipation of death.

A sad but graphic illustration of an animal seeking death, seemingly because of grief and despair, is offered in the story of Tom, a seven-year-old collie that belonged to Harold Myers of Houston, Texas. Harold and Tom were inseparable and it was understandable that the dog was lost without his master when Tom left home to join the armed forces during the Vietnam War. But, although Tom obviously was not happy with Harold's absence and moped a great deal alone, he seemed to accept the separation with resigned patience.

When Harold was killed in action, and from that day (several days before the Myers family was notified), Tom exhibited a determination to end his own life. Three blocks from the Myers home was a railroad track. Tom stretched himself across the track, but before a train arrived two men spotted him from the crossing and pulled him from the rail. But the following day the big collie stayed on the track until the train came. Did he somehow conceive that he would once again be with his master?

Tom's apparent suicide poses some interesting questions. If he had been killed on the first attempt, one could argue that the dog just happened to be on the track at the wrong time. Yet he was saved once, only to return. And if death was not his intention, he very easily could have moved out of the way. What understanding did Tom possess of life and death? He understood them clearly enough to choose one over the other. Was he too grief-stricken to go on? Did he believe he could join Harold on some plane of existence? And how did he know that Harold was dead? He made no attempts on his life until his companion was killed. Whatever our conclusions, we are faced with an understanding which allowed for choices.

Perhaps, as with people, death is an individual thing to be met by different animals in their own fashion. Some animals seem to be unaware of its approach, while others make preparations for the event. For example, certain dogs and cats search for places to be alone at the time of death, apparently aware that it is imminent.

Researchers have found that chimpanzees demonstrate a haunting fear of death. Dr. Adrian Kortlandt, who worked with primates in the Congo jungle for many years, found that chimpanzees will become quite frightened and draw back from dead animals. His provocative experiments will be described in a later chapter, but it might be noted here that chimpanzees not only demonstrate great fear of death but also do not handle well the death of a family member or companion.

In his account of the mountain gorillas of Kisoro, George Schaller relates how a young gorilla refused to leave the dead body of its adult companion. It was forced into the position of either escaping into the jungle in search alone for members of its group, a task for which it was not prepared, or clinging to the last vestige of its former happy group life, a dead leader who for the first time failed to protect it. The youngster was finally captured but died a short time later in the London Zoo.

One can compare this account with one by Robert Kastenbaum, co-author of *The Psychology of Death*, of an eighteen-month-old human child's first contact with death in the form of a dead bird. The child recognized it as a bird, "but he appeared uncertain and puzzled. Furthermore he made no effort to touch the bird. This was unusual caution for a child who characteristically tried to touch or pick up everything he could reach. David then crouched over and moved slightly closer to the bird. His face changed expression. From its initial expression of excited discovery it had moved to puzzlement: now it took on the aspect of a grief mask."

With both gorilla and human child we discover incomprehension of death at first contact with it. But a few weeks after David's first dead bird, Kastenbaum explained, he came across another, and his reaction to this was completely different. "He picked up the bird and . . . reached up toward a tree, holding the bird above his head. He repeated the gesture several times . . . accompanying his command now with gestures that could be interpreted as a bird flying." When putting the bird back in the tree several times failed to bring it back to life, the youngster accepted that this was not going to work. "He looked both sober and convinced" and then lost interest altogether.

Biologist Lyall Watson tells us in *The Romeo Error* that "no serious study has ever been made of death or death-awareness in any species other than our own, but there are anecdotal scraps and odd experimental findings that fit together to produce an astonishing pattern. As this picture takes shape, the notion of universal continuity begins to look less and less childish."

One of the first persons to breed chimpanzees in captivity, Rosalia Abreu, related to R. M. Yerkes, author of *Almost Human*, that upon the death of one of her female chimpanzees in a secluded enclosure, her mate, who was outside the park, began to scream. "He continued to scream, looking about as though he saw something." Later, when another chimp died, he did the same thing.

"He screamed and screamed and screamed," Abreu said. "And he kept looking and looking with lower lip hanging down, as if he saw something that we could not see. His scream was different from anything I have heard at other times. It made my flesh creep."

Watson notes that under some circumstances, animals seem to pay little attention to death but that there are some situations in which the ability to respond to dying has survival value. For example, after a lioness kills her prey and she and her group have eaten all they want, other animals move in to finish off whatever is left. Hyenas and jackals are most likely attracted to the site by sounds and smells, but Watson believes that vultures use some other cue and will locate a hidden corpse with great precision. Vultures have excellent eyesight and as soon as one spots food, others soon arrive, "but sometimes this just does not seem to be enough to explain their presence," Watson states. "I have seen vultures arriving in the dark to sit like impatient pallbearers around an antelope that had been shot, and on those occasions there were no mammalian scavengers around to attract their attention.

"I am not suggesting that vultures are able to diagnose death at a distance, but I do believe that in some situations a signal goes out from a dying organism and that this alarm is particularly strong when the attack on it is sudden and violent. It seems likely that the signal began as a warning and was originally intended only for members of the same species, but in time and evolution it has turned into an all-species SOS. Depending on the circumstances and the species involved, this signal can simultaneously be read as 'Help, I need assistance,' 'Look out, there's a killer around,' 'Relax, he's eating someone else,' or 'Come on, dinner's ready.' There is value in all these communications and economy in the fact that all are based on a single signal given by a single individual in trouble. I believe that there is now sufficient evidence to show that such a system does in fact exist."

What does a knowledge of death imply? If a creature

is aware that the occurrence of death eliminates mortal life, it suggests that this creature can project into the minutes, hours, or days ahead with the knowledge that the lost one will not return. There is the determination, however arrived, that an irreversible change has taken place. An acquaintance with the finality of death has been displayed by other species. When I was a boy growing up on a Kansas farm, we had a neighbor, T. J. Randle, who raised horses. He understood the workings of those horses like some people today understand computers. He could gentle-break tough customers better than anyone I have ever known. This feat was recognized by everyone in the area and people would say, "Ol' T.J. must be part horse himself . . . he understands them and they seem to understand him."

T.J. allowed his horses to graze around his house and there was a gate at the entrance to his drive that had to be opened and shut when driving in and out of his place. When he died and the ambulance came to pick up his body, all of his horses were quietly standing around the house. But when the ambulance bearing T.J.'s body exited through the gate, the horses also stampeded through it and headed up the road with the ambulance. Not wanting to hit one of them, the driver drove slow. He stopped once to ask a neighbor, following behind in his car, if something should be done about the horses. "Naw," the neighbor said. "They'll get tired pretty soon and go back." They didn't. They galloped the five miles to town and surrounded the ambulance while T.J.'s body was being moved inside the funeral home.

The sheriff's department was called about the horses and the sheriff said he would get some deputies to round them up before they caused an accident. But he didn't need to bother, for when they were next spotted they were already on the road leading back to the ranch.

"Telling the bees" was an ancient custom of letting the bees know when their beekeeper had died. Some times the beehive was draped in black crepe. Following the custom of telling the bees, when Sam Rogers, a cobbler and postman of the Shropshire village of Myddle, England, died, his children walked around his fourteen hives and told the bees. According to the Associated Press, April 1961, the relatives of Rogers gathered at his grave and shortly after they arrived, thousands of bees from Rogers's hives more than a mile away came and settled on and about the coffin. The bees entirely ignored the flowering trees nearby. They stayed for approximately half an hour and then returned to the hives.

A cat paid his respects at the grave of his master, according to a story in the autumn 1963 issue of *Tomorrow* magazine. The correspondent stated that his grandfather and a cat named Bill were extremely close. The cat followed him by day and slept in his bed at night. The man was seriously hurt in a railway accident and for a week lay in a hospital several miles from his home. He died in the hospital and his body was taken from there to the church and then to the churchyard for burial. As the rites were finished, an uncle of the writer looked up and saw Bill approaching the grave. He moved with dignity to the grave, stood for a short time looking at the coffin, and having paid his respects, turned and headed home.

An understanding of life and death and what it would take to keep the one from becoming the other was demonstrated a few years ago by a dog in Ohio.

On September 23, 1979, Rae Anne Knitter and Ray Thomas were hiking near Cleveland, Ohio, when Ray stepped out on a shale ledge to take a picture. The ledge gave way and Ray fell eighty feet to the hard ground below. His body stopped, however, on the edge of a small stream and he lay facedown in the water.

Rae Anne's mongrel dog immediately broke loose from her leash and ran to the edge of the cliff. A moment later she, too, plunged to the rocks below. Somehow she seemed to realize that there was not time for other options. Woodie broke both hips in the fall but managed to drag herself by her front paws to Ray's side and nuzzle his head out of the water.

When Rae Anne arrived at the scene, Woodie was

keeping Ray's head out of the water and he regained consciousness long enough to tell his fiancée, "I'm broken all over."

Rae Anne tried to put her hand under Ray's head but Woodie pushed her away. The girl summoned help and rescuers carried Thomas to an ambulance. It was also necessary to carry Woodie, for she could no longer move.

Thomas spent nearly three months in intensive care from a torn spinal cord, three broken vertebrae, and a broken left elbow and right wrist. But he acknowledged that "if it wasn't for Woodie, I'd be dead."

In addition to the broken hips, Woodie sustained fractures of seven toes. It took three months to recover from her life-saving leap. And today, according to Rae Anne, "She can't do some of the things she used to do, like sit up or chase a Frisbee. But she's okay and, thanks to her, so is Ray."

For her heroics Woodie was named the 1980 Ken-L Ration Dog Hero of the Year. She was awarded a gold medal, a gold-plated leash and collar, a one-thousand-dollar bond, and a pastry doghouse filled with dog food.

How many of us would have the courage to perform Woodie's feat? She must have known the extent of the risk. Dogs do not jump from heights which their bodies can't handle. Instinct or some inner knowing provides this caution. Yet Woodie, with only a second's calculation, plunged to the ground below. Even then, badly broken, she managed to drag herself to Ray's side.

It has been said that a dog is the only creature who has seen his God. Do dogs, and certain other animals, have this kind of adoration for humans? What kind of love would prompt them to risk their lives for us? Can we demonstrate a greater love? How can we argue that they have no knowledge of death when they demonstrate the importance of saving life?

Perhaps one could propose that the heroic animal is serving as an agent of a higher force. This is implied in the statement of a minister's wife whose dog saved her life: "God works in mysterious ways."

If the animal is acting as an agent of God, does this shift the decision-making away from the animal? Couldn't the questions be equally applied to any human performing unusual and superior deeds? In any case, doesn't the ability to listen and the willingness to act say something rather profound for the understanding and character of the animal? This issue will be explored later.

As with many humans, some animals seem unable to surrender a loved one to death. Devoted to this love, they cling to its memory as long as they live. Perhaps, like humans, they await the time of a reunion. This seemed to be the case with a female collie and one of her offspring.

I used to delight in Albert Payson Terhune's stories of his Sunnybank collies, and I recall Jean, who, contrary to most animal mothers, paid special attention to one of her puppies long after he was grown. She brought him the tastiest bits from her dish, took him bones, and even though he was larger than she, daily washed him from his head to the tip of his tail. Wherever Jock went, Jean was not far behind.

Then Jock got distemper and had to be isolated. This was before the days of antibiotics and, despite the struggle by Jock to survive and Terhune to save him, the big collie died. During Jock's quarantine, Jean refused to eat.

Jock was buried in a field more than a quarter of a mile away. The following morning, Jean was released and immediately she started searching every inch of ground, looking for her "puppy" and occasionally giving a sharp little bark that had always brought him running.

Finally she raced back for Terhune, her tail wagging. She caught hold of his coat and pulled him along to the mound that was Jock's grave. Jean lay down on the mound, her tail still wagging, knowing that Jock was close. Every day until her death years later, regardless of the weather, Jean visited Jock's grave, often staying for hours.

"Her waiting had no grief in it," Terhune explained. "It was full of gay hope."

Mr. and Mrs. Robert King, their small daughter, Mrs. King's elderly father, and a cat named Felix lived in the small town of St. Kildre in Australia. The old man died at the age of ninety and the cat couldn't be consoled. It roamed the house and·yard, searching and crying. They decided to take the cat for a ride in the hopes of distracting him.

Felix was quiet until they reached the outskirts of Melbourne when suddenly the hair on his back bristled, he trembled, and leaped through the car window and disappeared from sight in the traffic.

There was nothing the family could do but return home and hope that Felix would find his way on his own. The days passed and Felix didn't return. Then Mrs. King and her daughter visited the cemetery with some flowers and there, pacing back and forth on the top of the grave, was Felix. The cat was highly joyful at seeing them and started playing with the little girl as she had with the grandfather. The cemetery was ten miles from their home and more than five miles from where Felix had leaped from the car.

Twice the Kings tried to take Felix home, but each time they got as far as the cemetery gate the cat leaped from the car and scampered back to the grave. They made arrangements with the custodian for the cemetery to feed and care for the cat.

When John Hethington interviewed the family for *195 Cat Tales*, he drove out to the cemetery and there was Felix fixed like a sentry atop the grave. Hethington wrote: "This story haunts me. Perhaps it's because there are in it features that lie beyond the frontiers of human understanding."

"We can hardly expect to find certainties in this nebulous realm," Vincent and Margaret Gaddis told us in *The Strange World of Animals and Pets*. "Perhaps it is not so important what we believe as that we believe something and keep testing our beliefs. But upon one conviction we stand—that man cannot assign a surviving soul to himself and deny it to his animal brothers; that man and animal are creatures of instinct and reason with the difference one of degree and not of kind; and that if consciousness does survive, it is a quality of life itself and not of Homosapians.''

Interestingly enough, the farther we push the frontiers of human understanding, the more we suspect that what remains beyond the horizon far exceeds anything known. In a computer age of technological breakthroughs occurring daily, we breathlessly endeavor to form and cling to concepts, only to discover they are being hopelessly eroded by new research deluges even as we try to formulate them.

In no other area of scientific investigation is this more true than in the field of brain function, mind as something separate from the organic brain, and consciousness as a product of something other than neurological systems. The nature of awareness, its origins and extensions, can no longer be contained in the Procrustean bed of the old biological sciences. Both the rational and intuitive minds have escaped their dependency on the size and arrangement of the organic brain. Some scientists are even speculating that dependency is the other way around, i.e., the mind resides at a higher level of command and uses the brain as an instrument for information-processing and dissemination.

Not many years ago it was believed that intelligence could be determined by the size of the brain in comparison to body weight. When it was found that the human sometimes came in second in these comparisons, the theory was abandoned in favor of one that proposed that intelligence was determined not by the thickness of the cortex but on its folds and complexities. This schema of intelligence did rather well for a time until it was discovered that certain marine mammals held an edge over the human species in this department, coupled with findings that large sections of the brain could be destroyed without impairing intelligence.

Today, science is not so sure what constitutes intelligence, reason, consciousness. Dr. Elmer Green of Menninger's has even stated: "All of the body is in the mind, but not all of the mind is in the body." And as the models have crumbled so have our restrictive dogmas and we are faced with the possibility that consciousness does not occur by any known scientific structure. As limitations have been stripped from the human mind, we are open to new questions as to the nature of awareness and are somewhat startled to learn that we must extend these questions to creatures other than ourselves. Further, if the mind is not dependent on the physical brain, then the demise of the brain doesn't imply the same fate for the mind. The continued existence of the mind may well apply to any creature, human or otherwise, that possesses this quality. In any case, it is a provocative thought and one we will continue to pursue in the pages ahead.

CHAPTER TWO

Beyond the Brain

Anyone hesitant to assign reasoning abilities to Brutus, a suburb Chicago golden retriever/Irish setter mix, who found his way through busy city streets to get help from his veterinarian, may be resisting the facts.

Brutus had an earache and his owner, Barbara Barba of South Chicago Heights, took him to his veterinarian, Dr. Robert Mitchell of Steger, Illinois. The dog was treated for an ear infection and sent home with some medication. Ten days later, Barba took Brutus back for another treatment. These were the only times the dog had been to the clinic, and on both occasions he had been taken in a car.

Six weeks later, Brutus was put on his chain in the backyard, but one hour later Barba received a call from Dr. Mitchell, who told her that her dog was ready to be picked up. She told the veterinarian that it couldn't possibly be her dog as he was fastened in the backyard. A survey of the backyard, however, proved otherwise. She rushed to the clinic, to find Brutus waiting there for her, and was told by the waiting-room receptionist that the dog had entered the front door and had promptly sat down at the end of a long line of owners and their pets to patiently await his turn.

"Each time a dog went in to see the doctor, Brutus got up, moved over one place, and sat down again," the receptionist told news reporter Eric Brown. "He was so good that I simply assumed that he was with a lady who came in just after he did.''

Dr. Mitchell explained that when he had finished with his last patient before Brutus he ''went out into the waiting room to see who was next. Brutus walked right past me and went into the examining room. My mouth dropped open when I realized no one was with him. He cocked his head to one side, which is what dogs do when they have an ear infection.''

After he had treated Brutus, Dr. Mitchell checked the dog's ID tag and called his owner. She told the veterinarian that she was not aware that her dog's ear was still bothering him and that he had broken his chain in order to get help.

While not a great distance was involved, Brutus had to manage heavy traffic and find his way past hundreds of buildings in order to correctly select the Village Pet Clinic.

Veterinarian Dr. Michael W. Fox tells the story of a farmer friend who was keeping a pet coyote fastened in a kennel. The animal, nevertheless, became suspect when a number of chickens disappeared. One day, hiding out near the barn, the farmer saw the coyote take some of his food and some corn from a stored cache and lay them out as far from the kennel as its chain would allow it to go. Then it returned to its kennel to wait in hiding for its prey.

In the past, the coyote's manipulative behavior would have been explained away simply as instinct. But today, cases of animal behavior are causing more and more scientists to rethink their positions. Reports of insects camouflaging themselves in order to approach their prey, ants giving complex orders to co-workers, wolves using group tactics to trap other creatures—these have inspired a great deal of discussion on animal thinking. The National Zoo in Washington, D.C., has held large and important symposiums on the subject.

The major question, of course, remains: Can animals

think? Do they in fact demonstrate insight and foresight? Can they reason? Or is their behavior not to be attributed to intelligence but rather instinct?

Some animal behavior is instinctive or mechanical—a dog wagging its tail, a cat purring. But as Dr. Fox points out, when and to whom a dog wags its tail or a cat purrs, involves discrimination, choice. And the ability to discriminate—say, between a friend and a foe—involves the rudiments of intelligent reasoning.

"This is especially true when a dog wags its tail in order to influence, even manipulate, its owner for attention, food, play, or a walk outdoors," Dr. Fox explains. "Hasn't your cat all but led you to the refrigerator, begging for milk, or meowed to awaken you for its breakfast? Reasoning and insight underlie these complex actions; through them, an animal exhibits expectations, what it anticipates to be the outcome of its actions."

But the question remains as to whether animals are self-aware. According to the writings of two eminent scientists, *The Question of Animal Awareness*, by Dr. Donald R. Griffin, and *Animal Thought*, by Dr. Stephen Walker, we are told that, yes, to varying degrees, animals are in fact aware of themselves. While it is true that kittens and puppies will react to their mirror image as though it were another animal, when they mature, they begin to ignore the image, indicating that they have developed self-awareness.

The ability to think and reason, Dr. Fox points out, also entails the ability to make logical associations, and animals exhibit this. My dog hates to be sprayed for fleas with an aerosol can, and when I pick up a can for whatever purpose, he will quickly run and hide. A friend's spaniel will whimper when his mistress puts on perfume because he knows she is going to leave.

"And while it is difficult to know whether animals wonder or worry about things as we do, it is quite clear that they too experience anxiety and apprehensiveness," Dr. Fox said. "A sheltie I know, who recently went on a short but unpleasant plane ride, now has an anxiety attack, barking and running all over the place, any time a plane flies over her home. Such associative phobias are common in animals.''

There are persons who argue that animals can't possibly possess the ability to think because they lack verbal language. They may lack the means whereby they can produce verbal human language, at least as we are used to hearing it, but animals have proven their ability for intelligent communication. They use foresight (the ability to set goals) and hindsight (learning from experience) in carefully thought-out behavior. They have even been caught telling lies. Following is a sign-language conversation between Roger Fouts, a psychologist at the University of Oklahoma, and Nucy, a precocious chimp, after Lucy went to the bathroom on the living-room floor:

Roger: ''What's that?''
Lucy: ''Nucy not know.''
Roger: ''You do know. What's that?''
Lucy: ''Dirty, dirty.''
Roger: ''Whose dirty, dirty?''
Nucy: ''Sue's.''
Roger: ''It's not Sue's. Whose is it?''
Nucy: ''Roger's.''
Roger: ''No! It's not Roger's. Whose is it?''
Nucy: ''Nucy dirty, dirty. Sorry Nucy.''

In their book *Smarter Than Man?* Karl-Erik Fichtelius and Sverre Sjolander discuss a phenomenon they define as ''neoteny.'' Neoteny is a process that produces an organism whose fixed muscular responses and instincts have never been locked into the adult stage. Such an organism has a great range of possible combinations and recombinations, the authors explain, both in determining the sequence of muscle contractions and in coupling these contractions with incoming stimuli. Neoteny produces an individual who can do all sorts of things in a great many different ways, and whose behavior in any given situation is neither rigid nor stereotyped. The ease with which dolphins and human beings can be conditioned, and the great variety of their behavior, can be seen as examples of neoteny.

"Dolphins have many neotonic characteristics," Fichtelius and Sjolander state. "An obvious example is their undisguised joy and interest in play. In fact, it was the first captive dolphins themselves who took the initiative in a great many of the simple games now played between humans and dolphins in aquariums all over the world. Dolphins, even adults, can play for hours with a ball or feather. They are as tireless as human children in this respect."

Fichtelius and Sjolander point out that dolphins appear to play even in the wild state and have been observed many times riding the wakes of ships in ways that can hardly be classified as other than playful. Dolphins have been observed surfing, and individual dolphins were seen returning repeatedly to the same starting point in order to catch a new wave.

"In connection with the concept of neoteny, we might also discuss the relationship between intelligence and instinct," Fichtelius and Sjolander stated. "If by intelligence we mean a series of capabilities appropriate to a certain animal species in certain situations—and to some extent this is the definition we use in intelligence tests—then it can be argued that the intelligence we have measured may coincide with the animal's instincts. Take as an example of our attempts, in test situations, to account for the complex communications among bees about honey, or the dam-building of beavers. By means of instinctual control, these species find room for an astoundingly complicated program of action in a very limited cerebral space. Insects are completely dependent on such a solution. Their special, complex, and appropriate behavior does not admit of many alternatives. This is not what we mean by intelligence.

"At the other end of the scale are the neotonic animals, not guided by instinct, who must learn a whole series of complicated procedures from their parents, and who must be prepared to solve problems on their own. These kind of animals, whom we designate as intelligent, require a long time for maturation and learning. It is often said that human beings have the longest maturation period of any animal as regards to mental faculties. It seems, however, that the elephant takes at least as long. In captivity, an elephant is not considered fit for work until it is about twenty years old. How long it takes for a sperm whale to reach the same relative maturity is not known.''

The authors define intelligence as the ability to differentiate, to combine and generalize, to analyze and associate, to perceive continuity and arrive at the concept of cause and effect, to imagine the results of contemplated actions, to deliberate and find the means of reaching a desired goal.

Innumerable stories have been told about the bottlenose dolphin which point to this kind of intelligence, such as the following example.

Two dolphins in an aquarium were playing—or so it seemed—with an eel. The eel kept saving itself by swimming into a hole in the bottom of the pool. With this occurrence, one of the dolphins swam up to a small fish with a poisonous sting, took the fish carefully in its mouth, and shoved it into the eel's hole. Immediately the eel fled, was caught by the dolphins, and so the game went, according to Danish ethologist Holger Poulsen.

A team of researchers led by Dr. Gregory Bateson was able to teach a dolphin in a Hawaiian aquarium to perform one new trick after another in order to be rewarded. According to Bateson, the dolphin not only understood what was required of it, but also revealed great imagination and invention in adding to its repertoire.

Dolphins can reportedly learn by observation. In aquarium shows, it often happens that the dolphins expected to perform certain tricks fail to do so for reasons not always understood. Yet, dolphins untrained to do a particular trick have stepped in and performed it per fectly.

Oftentimes the question has been raised whether dolphins communicate with one another by some means that is comparable to human speech. The following experiment was carried out by Dr. Jarvis Bastian.

A female and male were presented with a signal light and two keys. When the light was steady they were to depress the key on the right; when the light was blinking, the key on the left. If they did it correctly, they would be rewarded with fish. This they learned very quickly. They then had to learn that the male was to press first or there would be no reward. A screen was placed between the dolphins so that only the female saw the signal light. When the first signal was given, the female swam up to her keys and made some dolphin sounds. The male then pressed the correct key of his pair, whereupon the female pressed the correct key on her side. The dolphins never failed to perform this trick correctly.

German Professor G. Pilleri writes that the dolphin's brain "attains a degree of centralization far beyond that of man." In the opinion of this scientist, ". . . the ultimate status of man's brain in the ranking of mammals is today beginning to be a matter of doubt."

If man should ever learn how to talk to dolphins, the physicist and biologist Leo Szilard has predicted, these "intellectuals of the sea" would win all the Nobel prizes for physics, chemistry, and medicine, and the Peace prize to boot.

When two dolphins talk to each other they appear to engage in actual dialogue. Several years ago, Dr. John Lilly, in his Institute for Communications Research on the Island of St. Thomas in the Antilles, provided somewhat convincing evidence of this when he divided a dolphin couple by a panel of sheet metal. Initially there was a shrill concert of whistles by both dolphins. They could recognize each other's voices but could not see each other. They tried unsuccessfully to leap high enough to see each other behind the partition.

They both sank into gloomy silence for a time. After a time, the male began encouraging his mate to engage in conversation. He talked for some time before she finally made a sound. At this, the male fell silent, and spoke again only after the female had finished. This went on for some time in constant alternations of sound for periods up to half an hour. But sometimes there would be a duet, when one dolphin chimed in with the other's whistles, sometimes loud, other times quietly.

Dr. Kenneth S. Norris, at the Makapuu Oceanographic Institute of Hawaii, made use of the dolphins' love for dialogue by having his Pacific dolphins talk by telephone with Atlantic members of the species in the marine laboratories in Miami. Communication via underwater microphone, public telephone cables, and an underwater loudspeaker for each of the participants yielded far better results than the experimenters had expected. In this case, too, each dolphin allowed the other to finish what he or she had to say before beginning to reply with gurgling and whistling sounds.

Professor Winthrop N. Kellogg of Florida State University reported in his book, *Porpoises and Sonar*, that he recorded dolphin sounds with underwater listening devices aboard his motorship. A curious fact he discovered was that a dolphin couple can chat even if each mate is separated by a considerable distance in the midst of a talkative dolphin school. Each dolphin always knows who is addressing whom. The one directly addressed replies in his turn and is not in the least bothered by the general conversation among the others. The scientists have dubbed this the "cocktail party effect."

Scientists examining the dolphins' communication systems are trying to decode their verbal and nonverbal signals. Researchers are working to determine how echolocation—the complex sonar communication system dolphins use to navigate—can be used to protect them from their greatest threat, the tuna net. Justin Kaplan, writing in *Omni* magazine, explained that cetacean scholars from Florida to Australia are studying the dolphins' complex familial and social relationships. In the laboratory, scientists are attempting to unravel the mystery of the dolphin brain, an organ quite different in function from man's "but with a creativity center larger than our own."

Many cetacean researchers agree that the person who has given scientific credibility to the field is psychologist Louis Herman, director of the University of Hawaii's Kewalo Basin Marine Mamman Laboratory. For the past decade Herman and his associates have worked with two Atlantic bottlenose dolphins, Phoenix and Akeakamai, testing their ability to understand and execute commands in two kinds of artificial language. Phoenix's language consists of electrically generated computer whistles. Ake's is based on hand and arm gestures. Each language has a "vocabulary" and a set of rules governing how the sounds or gestures are arranged in sequences that form thousands of sentences. Using these languages, Kaplan explains, Herman has shown that dolphins understand the meanings of the words in their languages and, even more important, how word order affects meaning. This ability is believed to be at the core of most human languages, a trait many scientists would argue is a sign of intelligence.

Herman has discovered, for example, that dolphins can differentiate between phrases such as "Pipe fetch surfboard"—which translates to "Get the pipe and take it to the surfboard"—and "Surfboard fetch pipe," which means "Get the surfboard and take it to the pipe."

The commands are issued in two different ways: through a set of computer whistles broadcast through an underwater speaker, and through a series of hand and arm gestures. For the latter, a trainer stands at the tankside, wearing dark glasses to control unintentional visual clues. The trainer then makes a series of gestures that construct a sentence.

Kaplan notes that "Herman contends that dolphins 'develop an understanding of the words of their language at the level of a concept.' For example, 'under' means 'passing beneath,' and dolphins will raise an object from the tank bottom to swim below in response to 'under.' He has also demonstrated that dolphins understand references to absent objects. When asked 'ball question,' which means 'Is there a ball in the tank?' Ake searches the pool and responds on a 'yes' or 'no' paddle. When the dolphin presses the 'no' paddle, it implies she had understood the sign, formed a mental image of the object referred to, and deduced the ball is not there. This ability—called referential reporting—has previously been documented only in apes and man.''

Herman's laboratory sounds more like an aviary than a marine habitat, filled with a cacophony of creaky clicks, squeals, and high-pitched whistles, according to Kaplan. A new venture will be to identify which dolphin is sending these signals and which is receiving them. It is a difficult task, as dolphin sounds are produced in the region of their blowhole and emitted through the head without any visible indication.

In a preliminary study conducted with Peter Tyack, an assistant scientist at Woods Hole Oceanographic Institute, Herman and associates attached to the head of a dolphin, using suction cups, a primitive contraption called a vocalite—a device developed by Tyack that lights up whenever a dolphin makes a sound. Along with the aid of Richard Ferraro, a scientist at the Institute of Applied Physiology and Medicine, Herman is developing and testing a more sophisticated device. A microcomputer, it is fastened by suction cups to the dolphin's head and records each sound and offloads the time of every vocalization into a second computer. The recordings will be analyzed to learn which dolphin was communicating, what the sounds were, and what behaviors were occurring at the time.

Kaplan explains that ''Scientists have known since 1965 that dolphins have distinctive signature whistles, which they use to identify themselves. Tyack's work showed that the animals were actually imitating one another's whistles. 'Learned mimicry is rare in the animal kingdom, but dolphins can be trained to imitate particular sounds, and wild dolphins appear to use this skill to imitate each other's whistles, perhaps to initiate social interaction,' says Tyack. With support from the Office of Naval Research in Arlington, Virginia, Tyack is studying the social function of the whistles by recording the sounds of captive dolphins at the New England Aquarium and Chicago's Brookfield Zoo.''

CHAPTER THREE

Everything Related to Everything

A new picture of life is unfolding. Until recently we have thought of life in terms of physical substance. Somehow, out of the bundle of mechanical and chemical properties, sprang our emotions and thoughts. This was the position of science and therefore the basis of most people's beliefs. While an opposing camp suggested that the mind was independent of the physical body and merely occupied it as a medium through which to function within material existence, this was a position reserved for the religious and metaphysically inclined. For the most part it was held that the secrets of life would need to be found within the atoms, molecules, and cells of living organisms.

How a physical body could have nonphysical functions was not clearly understood by science. Nor, on the other hand, were the theologians and metaphysicians able to explain adequately how the mind or spirit could act upon material substance. The explanations were indeed vague. If spirit and matter were both accepted as realities existing at either end of life's spectrum, they remained very much isolated in those positions, for the bridge between could not be found.

But apparently the construction of this bridge is now under way. Technological breakthroughs have provided scientists with the tools to examine things other than the mechanical and chemical properties of living organisms.

Investigators pursued smaller and smaller particles until, instead of talking about smaller and smaller objects, they spoke of vibrations, frequencies, waves. The various forms of life, instead of being a collection of units, took on the appearance of energy being in a constant whirl and moving in and out of transient structures. At the same time that cells and tissues could be seen as energy fields, it was also discovered that emotions and thoughts produced measurable energy. A common denominator between the material and the abstract had been established. It was no longer so difficult to imagine how mental stress could result in ulcers and malnutrition produce hallucinations.

The new research has revealed that living organisms have electrodynamic qualities. They receive and transmit various radiations and in doing so influence and are influenced by all divisions of the electromagnetic spectrum: gamma rays, X rays, ultraviolet light, visible light, infrared, short and long radio waves. These discoveries have launched scientist and philosopher alike into the investigation of the electrodynamic dimensions of life, and one of the most exciting outcomes of this adventure is the demonstration that the biological organisms can no longer be described as limited to a bag of chemicals. Living creatures can no longer be so confined, and emerging from this cocoon, they appear no longer imprisoned by space and time. This is exciting news, but equally provocative is the new evidence that the nature or pattern of any life form can be determined electrically before it becomes materialized in physical substance. This finding has far-reaching implications.

The evidence questions the currently accepted idea that the DNA molecule is life's master key. The new findings suggest that behind the chemistry and mechanics of molecules is an electrodynamic principle which precedes and determines physical form. Should future research continue to confirm this, the design for any form of life can be known prior to its materialization in physical matter. This would be the case whether we are considering creation, growth, illness, or whatever. We are suddenly observers of life at a level not previously available to us. One doesn't have to be an unground visionary to become excited about the new terrain awaiting exploration.

Electrophotography, sensitive voltmeters, tobiscopes, high-grain amplifiers, laser beams, holographs, force-field detectors, Schlieren devices, photomultipliers, biometers, auragrams, and other electrodynamic sensing devices being invented even while these words are being written are providing maps for a new kind of journey. Along the way, our vision of life, its magnitude, its potentialities, will surely be expanded, likely beyond anything our imaginations can now picture. This is not to seduce the reader into the illusion that all answers are contained herein. The evidence, however exciting and promising, is not exhaustive and it proffers many more questions than it offers answers. Yet the questions take on the greater virtue, for they push us beyond premature closure on issues which, for all but the most practical of purposes, will never be closed.

"Science no longer holds any absolute truths," biologist Lyall Watson tells us in *Supernature*. "Even the discipline of physics, whose laws once went unchallenged, has had to submit to the indignity of an Uncertainty Principle. In this climate of disbelief, we have begun to doubt even fundamental propositions, and the old distinction between natural and supernatural has become meaningless . . . I find this tremendously exciting. The picture of science as a jigsaw puzzle, with a finite number of pieces that would one day all be slotted neatly into place, has never been appealing. Experience indicates that things are not like that at all. . . ."

Science does, indeed, have soft edges. Twenty years ago few questioned that the involuntary nervous system was anything else but that. It was believed that certain functions of the body were automatic and not subject to voluntary control. Biofeedback—along with a few wandering yogis—have taught us otherwise. It wasn't too long ago that we discovered the size of the dolphin's cerebral cortex and we haven't been quite so comfortable with our superiority ever since. And now there are serious questions as to whether pain is only a matter of response of the nervous system or whether it is also an electromagnetic signaling below the cellular level and a process shared by all forms of life regardless of how primitive and even without the existence of any known nervous system. But this isn't science with a hard edge. This is a wandering through nature and life's experiences with doors and eyes open, capitalizing on whatever information comes into view as gleaned by whatever senses or tools we have on hand at the time. Such gatherings are tucked away, not as absolutes on a shelf, but as seeds for further sowing.

This is adventure at its best. It provides us with Prometheus's inclinations to climb the highest hills accessible to us without getting bound unduly to the fruits of our endeavor. The search can go on and we are not tied to what in the future may prove to be a nondefensible position. Laotse—that ancient Chinese sage who understood the foolishness of trying to capture blithe spirits in boxes—would approve.

In any case, we have largely envisioned the things of our universe to be objects—that is, the universe was a collection of large and small objects. We understood that all things could be broken down into various chemical components. A grain of sand was a simple and small amount of minerals; a planet was a complex and large collection of organic and inorganic material. We also understood that all matter could be further divided into atoms, and finally that that atom itself could be divided. But the more scientists studied particles of matter, the smaller they became, and the suggestion was made that any unit of matter cannot be understood as a static thing or object but as a dynamic process. Instead of matter being a thing as such, it became a movement. At this point many physicists started saying that the basic material of the universe was not matter but energy. What appeared to be objects, large or small, were energy fields.

That they appeared to have shape and substance was a "symptom" of the field or, in other words, the response of the observer to the field of energy. Since the observer was also a field of energy, his response was the reaction of one field of energy to another.

These findings were largely the result of the development of extremely sensitive instruments that could probe depths of perception beyond that normally available to our five senses. Just as the microscope took us into infinitely smaller worlds which we never knew existed before and the telescope opened the door to infinitely larger ones, so other instruments made us realize that our world of objects was one of limited appearances only. Closer examination, afforded by tremendous magnification and the monitoring of very high frequencies, provided the insight that our world of realities was essentially an illusion. The fact that we could live in, move about, and use that world of seeming objects didn't alter the nature of its greater reality, for we, too—our bodies, senses, etc.—were part of the illusion.

We think of our earth as being somewhat solid, and yet if the substance of the earth was as solid as that material at the center of a white star, it would have to be so condensed or compressed that it would be the size of an ordinary golfball. Yet the white star is not an absolute solid; it's just the most solid of which we are aware. Obviously, what we usually think of as being solid is mostly space. If it were possible for some intelligent being to live on a white star and for him to travel in space, when he came to the earth he would pass on through because to him it would be such a thin vapor he would not be aware of its existence.

Our senses tell us that the objects which we touch are at rest, and yet scientifically viewed, the objects are fields of electronic and protonic energies moving at prodigious speeds. Nothing in the universe is at rest, for even the particles of a rock are swarming in incessant motion. Examination reveals that our experience of the world is nothing more than our thoughts concerning it. Our world is in a state of ever-becoming rather than settled being; it is not so much of a structure as a flow. There is never a moment when the vibration of atomic energy comes to rest, and because of this nothing abides. It is in a constant state of change. This is the reason that science no longer describes nature as "things" but rather as "processes." Buddha explained that nothing remains the same for two consecutive moments and declared, "Whoever perceives in truth and wisdom how things pass away in this world, in his eyes there is not 'It is' in this world."

With the demise of the old belief in the ultimate nature of matter existing in space, the new physics declared that matter was not the last substance. Atoms were divided and found to be waves, and theory of relativity and quantum mechanics revealed that the world's stuff is but a series of happenings.

The new physics and the rapid advance of technology opened the door to the investigation of nature as energy fields, waves, and frequency. The new instruments provided the means to explore—along with the other expressions of nature—the nature of man himself. If he, too, was not a thing but a happening, he could no longer be contained in a time-space structure. What were his dimensions? If he was an energy field, how did he react to and with other energy fields? The readings from a variety of instruments made it clear that the human body radiated energy fields for some extended distance. Such findings paved the way for science to become legitimately involved in the study of man's extended states of being.

For as far back as history can remember, persons seeming to have unusual perceptive powers have claimed they were not limited in time and space—they could see the future as well as the past, could communicate with receptive persons at any distance, and influence their environment by the control of the force fields of which the universe was constructed. Such matters, however, might be all right for magicians, occultists, and poets, but they were hardly fare worthy of serious and practical scientists. But with everything reduced to energy, this was a different ball game. With objects taken out of their boxes and being no longer contained as configurations, their interaction or influence upon one another could be almost anything. Explorations were launched to discern what these interactions were and how they could take place.

Along the road, mind was defined as something apart from and more than the organic brain. Freed from its wrappings, the mind was traced as being able to move backward and forward in time; it could travel to some distance and report on events; it could deliver or receive a message with no assistance beyond its own power. Seeing and hearing were no longer the sole domain of the eyes and ears and could occur quite apart from either sense. Electrophotography and energy-field detectors of various sorts monitored subtle forces radiating from the human body that might explain how healing, such as the laying on of hands, might take place, how the growth rates of plants are affected, how physical objects are moved without so-called physical force, etc.

"In the world, systems of occult physics is a concept of energy and a related field theory, remarkably similar to that of modern physics. Namely, there is one primary form of energy from which everything else is constructed," Dr. Elmer Green, director of the Psychophysiological Laboratory at the Menninger Foundation in Topeka, Kansas, stated. He added, "In occult physics, however, it is postulated that the elaborated structure of the one basic energy includes not just physical substance, mental substance, and other more rarified materials, and that in the human being all these materials are brought together."

Sir Aurobindo, the Indian philosopher and teacher, wrote that "one can think of the universe as all spirit, with matter being the densest form, or one can think of the universe as all substance, with spirit being its most rarified form."

The wide acceptance of the body as an energy field radiating forces beyond the perimeters of the body has initiated a new field of medicine—bioelectrics. Bioelectrical medicine has gained public attention through acupuncture, auricular therapy, electrical stimulation, and sedation of the muscles, organs, and brain; electrophotography of the radiation surrounding the body, a process that promises to be effectively used in the diagnosis of disease; and the electromagnetic stimulation of healing and growth, although the demonstration of the latter has been largely confined to small animals at this writing.

But the implications of the world as energy goes far beyond the field of bioelectric medicine as it is now understood. If all life forms have no real limitation in time and space and everything can affect everything, then we are faced with the awesome conclusion that states of physical, emotional, and mental health are subject to alteration by energy fields both close at hand and extended to an unknown distance in space. All living creatures affected by each other as well as other environmental factors, and the task of sorting through and measuring these forces, seems nigh overwhelming. Nonetheless, this assignment appears mandatory if we are ever to comprehend the array of forces working for and against our well-being. Within this model, health is not simply the control of germs, viruses, etc., and the proper care of the body through nutrition, exercise, etc., but truly a holistic matter involving the state of everything in the universe. If the ecology is out of balance, for example, one's health may likewise suffer. By the same reasoning, if one's health is out of kilter, it may affect the ecology. According to this position, events or states do not occur in isolation.

Yet, as we could no longer consider the universe as constructed of particles and started talking in terms of energy, so energy, as the catchall term for everything happening in the world, is now presenting us with some problems. When we speak of energy we are generally referring to the forces of nature, which are four in number: electromagnetism; the force that holds subnuclear particles together inside the nucleus of each atom; radioactivity; and gravity. If we use the eastern concept of prana, chi, or vital energy as the universe force in which everything moves and has its being, the definition may be broad enough to incorporate everything imaginable in our world. But within the scientific tradition, all phenomena were contained within one or another of the four forces of nature, and its behavior was explained according to the known laws of physics.

The problem which has evolved concerns phenomena with demonstrable and measurable results that cannot, however, be explained according to the laws of physics. True, sensitive instruments have recorded electromagnetic fields emanating from life forms, including the human one, and these may explain some of the phenomena. But many of the so-called psychic phenomena are not predictable according to these rules. Considerable efforts have been made to block telepathic PK powers, for example, with Faraday cages, reversed electromagnetic fields, etc., to no avail. Efforts to define the carrier wave for healing forces over long distances have also failed. Perhaps we do not understand as much as we thought about the four forces of nature. On the other hand, we may be dealing with some kind of psi field with laws other than those known.

Dr. Jule Eisenbud states in his book, *The World of Ted Serios*: "However, quite apart from the formidable difficulties not only of quantifying the kinds of information involved but of identifying, isolating, tracking, and measuring the role of various factors conceivably involved in their 'transmission,' some investigators are dubious on general theoretical grounds that present-type physical hypotheses are at all applicable to psi phenomena. . . . Pascual Jordan, Professor of Theoretical Physics at the University of Hamburg, after surveying the field, concluded that there are no types of radiations now known or that could ever be known to physics that could account for the phenomena in their variety and entirety. The latter has declared flatly . . . that physical research 'has to give up physics as a basic means of clarification.' "

Not all scientists have given up the search of an explanation for psi phenomena within the confines of physics. As Eisenbud comments in a footnote: "The Russians, as might be expected, have not completely abandoned the question of the energetic nature of psi phenomena as a futile problem. Vasiliev, noting the rapidly mushrooming discoveries of nuclear physics, is loath to rule out the possibility that 'sooner or later a new macrofield will be discovered which will go beyond the boundaries of atoms and engulf surrounding space.' He lays great store in the future development of information theory, which may render obsolete some of the earlier energetic conceptions."

Perhaps, somewhere along the way, we will have to agree with Aurobindo that the problem is one of semantics and acknowledge the mystic's view of the world as being of one substance.

In *Wisdom of the Overself*, Paul Brunton points out that "the scientists who had discarded belief in matter still believe in energy. The latter has become their ultimate 'stuff.' But the energy out of what they would derive the world is as uncertain as matter. For when we ask for its production we get only its supposed 'transformations,' that is, sound, heat, light, etc. We do not find a pure energy-in-itself. Why? Because it is a conceptual creation useful only for practical purposes. Scientists have never perceived it. All they have perceived of it are its appearances of sound, light, heat, etc., but never the isolated energy itself. As a detectable reality, it is still uncatchable as matter. As a mathematical theory for practical purposes and as a calculator's symbol for technological purposes it takes a useful place, but it is still a supposition. It is supposed to work behind the universal movement, but it has never yet been exposed to view."

What we are apparently looking for is a cause with sufficient magnitude that it can encompass all of the effects of which we are aware. An explanation is offered by the world-famous astronomer Dr. Gustaf Stromberg, who states in his article "The Autonomous Field":

"When we say that force fields are autonomous we mean that they are not caused by particles, like electrons and photons. It is obviously difficult to picture a field which cannot be attributed to something else. We naturally look for a cause of the field; something beyond the observable effects. This 'something' must be of a very profound nature, since it must in some way or other be associated with the ultimate origin of energy, matter, life, and mind."

In concluding the article, Dr. Stromberg states: "The theory of the autonomy of force fields leads to the result that such fields can be analyzed into integral coherent units, and that this theory then makes it possible to understand many phenomena which the classical field theory is unable to explain. Principal among these phenomena are the wave nature and particle nature of matter and radiation and the small-scale and the large-scale organization in the living world. The theory has been shown to be a natural consequence of modern wave mechanics. It is also in harmony with recent discoveries in biology and gives us a new concept of life. It is directly opposed to the mechanical concepts which have until recently characterized natural science. It points directly to a world intimately connected with our own consciousness."

Scientists of the nineteenth century boasted that they alone could deal with the real world, but the scientists of the twentieth century have had to admit that they deal only with a world of abstractions. They have found that they are handling only some particular characteristics of a thing and not the thing itself. Science is quickly arriving at the point, according to Brunton, when its own facts and reasoning will force the conclusion "that the world-stuff is of the same tissue as that out of which our own ideas are made. It will then be seen that energy is not the prime root of the universe, that ultimate reality being mental in character cannot be limited to it and that it is but one of the chief aspects of this reality and not an independent power in itself. Energy will be found, in short, to be an attribute of mind, something possessed by mind in the same way that the power to speak is possessed by man. . . . If we see a thing at perfect rest and science tells us it is really in a state of perpetual restlessness, then we are entitled to conclude that the anomaly is caused by the limitations of our own perceptions which in the end are only our own consciousness. The stability which we see cannot be anything else than a mentally constructed one. We are entitled to relegate the thing's actuality to the realm where it must have always been, namely, of the mind.''

According to the principles of relativity, each ''thing'' is an appearance, and this implies the existence of some conscious being to whom it appears. How can the green grass and the blue water be thought of at all unless they are thought of as being seen? And how can anything be seen at all, Brunton asks, unless it is seen in someone's consciousness? The principles of relativity explain that consciously or unconsciously, the observer is always there in every act of perception and in every act of description. Even when we think of a time when the earth was uninhabited, we are thinking of the planet in terms of some mind's perception of it; it would seem impossible for us to do otherwise. One can think of no existence that is not known existence.

Brunton explains that it is a misconception of the position of mentalism, in which everything is viewed as a mental construct, to assert that the world does not exist when ''we are not thinking of it or that a mountain disappears when there is no man to behold it but revives again when somebody is present! . . . What mentalism really asserts is that the world's existence in itself without a knowing mind alongside it can never be established. Every materialist unconsciously assumes the presence of such a mind when he assumes that the world can exist independently. A world which is not an object of consciousness has yet to be found. Even when he thinks the world away from himself and foolishly believes that it is still present independently of a percipient mind, he is quite unaware of the fact that he is setting up an invisible spectator to whom it must appear as the world. Let him try to talk of a bygone planetary scene or an unvisited polar region without talking of it in terms of some being's perception of it; the feat cannot be done.''

Later, Brunton asserts that the materialist errs in believing ''that when the mentalist denies the existence of matter he also denies the existence of things and people or else turns them into mere spectral ghosts of their former selves. On the contrary, he says that they are certainly there. And he admits that they are present not within our heads but outside them. Only, he points out, they are mentally made. He does not deny the existence of solids, liquids, and gases. Only, he remarks, they are mental existences. He accepts the feeling of resistance and the touch of pressure as indicating the presence of a solid body but declares that these feelings are really sensations of the mind itself.''

These arguments were limited to the field of philosophy—fit fare for mellow conversations on cold winter nights—until recently. One could converse on these matters to his heart's content, take any position he desired for the sake of argument, and it really wasn't going to change his life to any noticeable extent. This may no longer be the case. Science has demonstrated that consciousness is the principal agent of change. With thoughts as things, the investigation of the nature of consciousness has become to a growing number of scientists the only game in town. How to enrich and elevate consciousness as the means of changing life for the better is quickly becoming the goal of educators, theologians, some behavioral scientists, and the central thrust of the human growth movement everywhere. On the other hand, mind control and manipulation are seen by others as the weapons of the future.

The significance of a world in which thoughts are things has vast implications in any direction we turn. With the sensitive instruments of the new technology clearly revealing that our thoughts alter our bodies, the bodies of others and all life forms, and our environment, then this is no longer an abstract theory gathering dust on some forgotten shelf but the focal point of tomorrow's human experience.

That the universe in the final analysis is consciousness would seem to have been demonstrated by polygraph expert Cleve Backster when his experiments with plants revealed an ability of the plants to react to the energy generated by humans, animals, and other plants. Backster wired a philodendron plant to some polygraph equipment to see whether he could measure the rate at which water rose from the roots to the leaves. To his amazement, he observed an unusual tracing, very similar to a reaction pattern of a human being under strong emotional stimulation. Knowing that human subjects have radical responses when their well-being is threatened, Backster wondered if he couldn't elicit a similar response from the plant. He decided to threaten to burn the leaves with a match . . . but before he could carry out the threat and, as a matter of fact, at the very moment the thought occurred to him, the plant responded with such force the needle almost jumped off the script recorder. The plant was responding to his thoughts.

This experiment has been successfully repeated by Backster a number of times and also by others. Backster, an international polygraph authority who has created lie-detector systems for the CIA and law-enforcement groups around the world, continued his experiments. In carefully controlled experiments, he discovered that plants not only respond to mental threats to their well-being but to feelings of love and thoughts of praise as well. He also found they can monitor conditions of life around them. Backster and an associate developed a double-blind electronic feedback system in which living shrimp were randomly dumped into boiling water by remote control. The experimenters had no way of knowing in which rooms the shrimp were being killed. Their only clues were readings from the plants that were hooked to polygraph machines in each room. When the shrimp were dumped into the water, the instrument registered a strong reaction from the plant in the same room.

"It would appear," Backster told me later over early-morning coffee, "that when cell life dies it broadcasts a signal to other living cells."

Backster's research with communications between many kinds of organisms led other scientists, who confirmed his findings, to believe that Backster had detected a communication signal that links all living things. Backster referred to it as primary perception below the cellular level.

Influenced by Backster's experiments, IBM chemist Marcel Vogel, using IBM's powerful electron microscope at San Jose, California, produced hundreds of photographs revealing that thought could affect changes in microscopic life forms. While psychology and psychosomatic medicine have been saying all along that thought can change physical patterns, they did not propose that thought changes extended beyond the boundaries of the subject himself. Apparently, if we can believe Backster, Vogel, et al., thought forces are not the respecters of space limitations.

If consciousness within life forms, human and otherwise, exists within the matrix of universal consciousness, then there is no actual separation as such. The visible expression of this consciousness would be energy appearing to take on various forms but having no separate or isolated existence. Within this model, the thought of healing is an energy field, or the thought of bending a spoon is the use of what appears to be a different energy force from doing the same thing with one's hands, also an energy force. Precognition would not be a matter of envisioning some event to be materialized in the future but rather an expansion of consciousness that allows for a greater understanding of universal consciousness in which all events and activities exist in the eternal present. Space and time concepts, within this model, would be the boundaries of the finite mind.

Research of consciousness continues to move us closer

and closer to the mystic's view of the world in which everything is related to everything else. According to this tradition, the higher mind, or greater consciousness, lies in the direction of the intuitional mind, the channel of direct perception of causes as compared to the rational brain's cognitive processing of effects. While neuroscience has tentatively placed intuitive functions within the right hemisphere of the brain, the consensus of the research to date would indicate the intuitional mind channels through this section of the physical brain rather than having its existence residing therein.

Where is the study of consciousness taking us? ''This exploration of the farther reaches of human consciousness typifies a new kind of mind research, already well begun,'' Dr. Jean Houston, director of the Foundation for Mind Research, has stated. ''Scientists, psychologists, and technicians of every stripe are gathering together with priests, shamans, mystics, artists, madmen, healers, and yogis, in conferences, academic seminars, laboratories, and ashrams, in a curious blending and interchange of ancient gnosis with contemporary knowhow. The result is a strange yeasting of East and West, science and ritual, the distant past and emergent future. The science of man is thus becoming richer than what we used to call psychology.''

In many ways, the interface mechanism between the mechanomorphic model of biological systems and the new vision of life forms with vast potentialities has been the discovery of his electrical dimensions. Within this realm the scientist and mystic can meet and communicate. Each has discovered this state through his own methods and approaches. Though not compelled to do so, they can use each other to test and confirm their findings. A mutual respect has evolved and the scientist—for the first time in several centuries—can correspond with the nonscientist without risking his credibility. The scientist can emerge from his self-imposed exile from all but physical parameters. Much as a child filled with wonder, he can speak of spirit, values, love, hope without losing his membership in the scientific community. Those qualities, so long outside the realm of scientific investigation, are being defined in terms of force fields—they are recordable and so were real. And the subjective state, because its influence of substance was measurable, is no longer the unwanted stepchild of objective data. They are rejoined as members of the same family. The experimenter is no longer isolated from the experiment. In a world where "things" no longer exist and everything, in any case, is related, all creatures are part of the circuitry.

All life forms are extended beyond the boundaries of the physical body . . . this is the Pandora's box opened by the new field of bioelectrics. The genie has escaped from his bottle and the lid was dematerialized in the explosion. Physical substance and its parent energy are both born of mental constructs and the poet's dreams have become as real as the sculptor's hammer.

CHAPTER FOUR

Something More Than a Dog

Scientist Henry Beston once noted: "We need another and wiser and perhaps a more mystical concept of animals. At present, we see their whole image in distortion. We patronize them for their incompletedness, for their tragic fate of having taken form so far below ourselves. And therein, we err, and greatly err. For the animal shall not be measured by man. In a world older and more complete than ours, they move finished and complete, gifted with extension of the senses we have lost or never attained, living by voices we shall never hear. They are not brethren, they are not underlings: they are other nations, caught with ourselves in the net of life and time, fellow prisoners of the splendor and travail of the earth."

These words take on particular significance when we try to understand the profound mystery of Missie, a Boston terrier who defied everything we have been led to believe about animals. Although we may not fully comprehend her life, her unusual behavior, nor perhaps even her identity, to study her life leaves us with the kind of questions not easily dismissed by the usual answers as to what animals are supposed to be.

Accurate prophecies of natural catastrophes, political races, moon landings, world events, and even the moment of birth and death—these are a few of her accomplishments. In comparing the successes of various prophets in recent years, the London *Daily Mail* called her "the best psychic in America." This would be no small achievement for a clairvoyant, but how humbling that the position would be reserved for a dog . . . or was she? The story of Missie is a strange one and impossible to forget.

We have to deal with Missie; however we might try to explain her talents, she cannot be ignored. Her case has been too well documented, too many times witnessed and recorded to shrug off as a tale constructed by deluded reporters. What makes it so difficult to analyze the highly unusual activities of Missie is that her behavior doesn't fit our models of what a dog can and cannot do. It is generally accepted that dogs can be psychically aware in a way that humans cannot, that dogs are so in tune with life they can make their way across a continent to locate a lost family, even keep in touch with their owners telepathically. We can struggle with these accomplishments and with only mild bewilderment adjust our model a bit and yet keep it together. But a four-legged creature that can see the future, even to predicting the hours of its own death, and had such extrasensory powers that it could run through a whole deck of cards without making a mistake—a feat no human can boast—somehow leaves us a little breathless.

Knowing that I was doing some writing on animals, James Grayson Bolen, former publisher of *Psychic*, sent me an article that had appeared in the magazine. It was written by Gina Cerminara, Ph.D., and was entitled, "Missie, the Psychic Dog of Denver."

Familiar with Dr. Cerminara's writing, I started the article with enthusiasm. After a few paragraphs, I was a mite stunned. I decided to get some more coffee. By the end of the article, the traffic in my mind was a bit congested; I was having difficulty sorting out concepts. I decided to sleep on it. The following day I reread the article and tried adding it up in my mind. I concluded that neither *Psychic* magazine nor Dr. Cerminara would present to the reader anything but the facts as received and understood by them. This being the case, they either did not have all the facts and there was some other explanation than clairvoyancy for Missie's accomplishments, or this dog was forcing upon us a complete reevaluation of intelligence and knowledge, even the nature of life itself. That night I called the dog's owner.

Miss Mildred Probert was charming, and we talked for quite some time. She was pleasant, intelligent, well informed, and quite down to earth. I think maybe I expected her to be otherwise. She discussed her pet's activities and unusual accomplishments in a rational but matter-of-fact way. I was impressed and more convinced that whatever Missie was, she was not to be lightly dismissed.

More calls followed; we exchanged letters, and several months later my wife Jeann'e and I paid a visit to Miss Probert at her home in Denver. An old Victorian-style home, it was filled with antiques, many of which her grandfather had brought over from his castle in Denmark. We were greeted at the door by a Boston terrier—not Missie, for she has been dead for several years. This dog's name was Sissie, a cousin of Missie, and Miss Probert quickly informed us that Sissie was not in any way psychic. She was delightful, nonetheless, and psychic enough to know that we loved dogs.

Sitting on the large, comfortable, overstuffed divan, with the mementoes of Missie—photos, clothes, toys, scrapbooks—strewn about us, we listened enchanted and amazed as the story of Missie unfolded. Miss Probert has told of her famous dog many times, to visitors, newspapers, and on radio and television, but there was not the slightest effort on her part to skip important details. She knows that she was blessed by a gift, one that changed her life and one that can have considerable significance for mankind. There was not the slightest pretense about our hostess. She was sincere and candid, and her great love for her departed companion was obvious and touching.

Even the way Missie came into her life was unusual. Miss Probert had been a floral designer for a number of years, and for a time had been manager and part owner of a pet shop. Ill health had forced her into retirement, but she took in animals that needed special care or boarded them when their owners were out of town. One day she was given a tiny newborn Boston terrier to care for. It was too small to be left in the litter. Its birth was odd. The mother had been delivered of three puppies by the veterinarian and all went well until midnight some hours later—when the mother dog went into convulsions of pain. She was taken to the hospital and operated on, and high near the rib cage the veterinarian located a tiny unit of flesh which he first thought to be some kind of unwanted growth; but it was found to be a puppy.

Missie never knew her mother nor her brothers and sisters. She knew only her human mother during the early stages of her life and, strangely enough, never grew to care for other dogs, preferring the company of people. She was extremely small for a Boston terrier, and there was a startling difference between her and other members of her breed. Boston terriers have dark, almost black eyes, but Missie's eyes were a deep cobalt blue. A few breeds of animals have light-blue eyes, but quite unlike Missie's.

Missie was nearly five years old before her psychic talents were discovered. Miss Probert, her mother, and Missie were out walking one day and they came upon an acquaintance with her small child in tow. They asked the youngster to tell them his age. When he didn't answer, the mother said that he was timid but he was three. Miss Probert leaned over the child and said, "Three. Say 'three.' " The child remained silent, but Missie suddenly barked three times. Everyone laughed and Miss Probert said, "Okay, smarty, how old are you?" Missie barked four times. More than a little surprised, Miss Probert asked, "How old will you be next week?" Five distinctive barks was the reply, which was correct.

"That was the beginning," Miss Probert told us. "It really wasn't a matter of my training her, for she knew things that I didn't. It was just a matter of trying to find out what she knew. It seemed endless." They tested Missie with fingers, asking her how many were being held up, and it was soon discovered that she could add. When she was asked such questions as "If I hold up four fingers and then five more, how many fingers will that be?" back would come the immediate and accurate response.

Miss Probert doesn't know how Missie learned to cope with numbers. "She developed her system entirely on her own. If a series of numbers was involved, such as a street address or telephone number, she would bark so many times for the first number, pause, bark out the second number, pause, and so on. She gave out a strange little muffled sound for 'zero.' "

Missie's uncanniness with numbers included not only addition and subtraction, but the number of letters in a word or name. Her extrasensory powers were discovered when a stranger to both Missie and her owner asked the dog to tell him his address. She barked out the numbers with hesitation. Miss Probert found that she could ask Missie to tell her how many letters were in the first name of a person she herself didn't know. Missie would bark out the correct number and would follow this with the last name.

On one occasion Missie was asked to give the number of letters in a woman's first name. Missie barked four times for "Mary." "How many letters are there in 'Merry' as in 'Merry Christmas'?" Back came the five barks. "How many letters in 'marry' as when two people get married?" Five barks again. Missie was constantly being tested on the number of letters in words, and she could invariably give the correct answer. She could do this whether or not Miss Probert was in the room, and she was tested in five languages. It is not known how many languages she was adept in, for she was tested only in five.

At parties, Missie could be relied on to tell people how many coins were in their purses or how many beans were in a sack. Usually those present did not know beforehand the number involved.

Dr. Cerminara tells in her article how during one party Missie was asked to give the number of spots on a playing card as it was held up. "He held the card in such a way that the back of the cards faced the dog and the assembled company. . . . This was the first time that Missie had ever seen a deck of playing cards, and yet she went through the entire deck without a mistake. Since nobody in the room saw the face of the cards until after Missie barked the response, at which time the experimenter showed the card to everyone, this would seem to preclude the possibility of telepathy and make it a clearcut case of clairvoyance. (When she came to a jack, queen, or king, she whined; then she was asked, 'Is this a picture card?' She barked three times for yes. Is it a king? Queen? Jack? She would bark yes when he came to the correct one)."

Missie figured out her way of answering yes and no. In addition to barking three times for yes and twice for no, she managed to sound out a distinguishable "uh-huh" for yes and "huh-uh" for no. For example, for yes she would say "Uh-huh, woof, woof, woof!" She also shook her head up and down for yes and sideways for no.

The small dog had health problems all of her life, including epilepsy, yet she had a great determination to live. "She enjoyed life so much and her great enthusiasm for everything that was going on around her was infectious. One time when she had to enter the hospital for an operation, I asked the doctor what ward she would be in. He said he didn't know, but Missie barked five times. The doctor said he didn't think she would be in that ward, but Missie was right.

"She could give you the correct serial numbers on dollar bills and the day, month, and year people—friends or strangers—were born. A physician we met was very skeptical of Missie's powers; he just wasn't going to be convinced. I finally said to him, 'Well, Doctor, there is one number that neither Missie nor I know and that is your private home number.' 'Oh,' he said, 'I never give that to anyone.' 'Go ahead,' I said to Missie, 'and tell us the doctor's private number, but we don't wish to hurt him so don't give us the last figure.' When she did it, he just leaned back in his chair, perplexed. On another occasion I asked a doubting newsman, 'What is your social security number?' 'I don't remember,' he said. 'What is this gentleman's social security number, Missie?' When she was right, he became a believer. You see, people looked for the gimmick and in the end found there wasn't any. I never knew how she could do these things and was as perplexed as anyone over her achievements.''

The small terrier's first psychic prediction was made on October 15, 1964, just before the elections and when everyone was pondering the outcome of the presidential race. Mildred had carried Missie into a local store where the clerks always enjoyed asking the dog questions. By way of conversation, Mildred said to the owner of the store, ''Well, how many weeks until the election?'' But before she could answer, Missie barked three times, which was correct. Taken somewhat aback, Mildred queried, ''How many days until the election, Missie?'' The correct nineteen barks followed.

At this point the owner said, ''Ask her who will win the presidency.'' ''But how could she know that?'' Mildred objected. Several people in the store had gathered around Mildred and her dog and they insisted that she ask Missie the question. ''If Mr. Johnson is one and Senator Goldwater is two, who will win the election?'' Mildred asked. One bark followed. Mildred reversed the question. ''If Barry Goldwater is one and Lyndon Johnson is two, who will win the election?'' Missie barked twice.

Someone present at this gathering phoned the *Rocky Mountain News*. A reporter and photographer were sent out and on November 8, 1964, a picture appeared in the paper of Missie, along with her prediction.

Many political predictions were to follow, but the only questions she ever refused to answer was whether Johnson would seek a second term. ''She just pushed out her little mouth and refused to answer,'' Mildred said. She predicted that Nixon would win the presidency, and she prophesied the outcome of many state and national political races, several that appeared very unlikely at the time.

Missie predicted the number of delays in the launching of Gemini 12, space probes, moon landings, and UFO sightings. On New Year's Eve of 1965, she was interviewed on KTLN, a Denver radio station, and after correctly barking the number of letters in "Happy New Year," she was asked, "When will the New York transit strike end?" She barked out January 13, and this proved to be correct. There had been some concern in the Denver area about an earthquake and Missie was asked if it was caused by natural phenomena. She answered no, and when asked when the real cause would be known, she said that it would be June. Sure enough, during that month it was learned that the cause of the quake was the result of the Army placing waste material from nerve gases into an old well, and the resulting explosions were thought to be the quakes.

The following day, January 1, 1966, the terrier with the penetrating blue eyes was on another radio station and predicted nine months in advance the outcome of the World Series, the day the series would end, and the correct score.

Missie's knowledge of future events seemed as vast as the imagination of those asking the questions. She foretold in her own ineffable fashion the failure of the atom-smashing plant to be located in Denver, the date for the initiation of the Paris Peace Talks and their outcome, and the return of the Colorado National Reserve from the Vietnam War.

A letter from Gary Robinson to Mildred but addressed "To Whom It May Concern" read:

"When I was a moderator on a radio talk show on station KTLN, Denver, Colorado, I had a phone call from Mildred Probert on September 30, 1965 (the day my baby girl was born). Miss Probert told me her 'psychic dog,' a Boston terrier, had been barking out a 'yes' answer, when asked if my baby would be a girl.

"This call was made before the baby was born.

"She put the dog on the phone to bark out the hour of time it was then and the temperature (which I checked with a phone temperature call).

"Missie also gave the date, Miss Probert asking 'What month, date, year, and the day of the week?' And how many letters in my name? All without error. It brought me a rush of calls when I remarked it was 'the first time I talked to a dog and it answered back.'

"After that, Missie performed over the phone on my program seven or eight times. Giving scores of forthcoming football games and the World Series baseball games, correctly.

"On New Year's Eve 1966, she gave answers for events occurring each month for the next year. All turned out to be true."

In many instances, Missie predicted the birth date, sex, and weight of an unborn child, including the birth of a girl to the Queen of Greece. Mildred stated, and the story is also told by Dr. Cerminara, that on one of these occasions, September 10, 1965, a pregnant woman stopped to visit with Missie and Mildred as they sat on their front lawn. Mildred mentioned the dog's ability to give correct data as to births. "Well," the woman replied, "I know what to expect concerning mine. I've lost two babies while carrying them and I have an appointment for a Caesarean operation for October 6."

"Will this lady have her baby on October 6?" Mildred asked Missie. No, the dog replied, whereupon the woman became quite upset, thinking that this meant the baby would die as her other babies had. Immediately Mildred asked if the baby would be alive and Missie barked three times for yes.

"In what month will the baby be born?"

"I already know that," the woman objected. "October."

"No," Missie barked, and followed this with nine

barks, meaning September. She then proceeded to bark twice, a pause, and then barked eight times for the twenty-eighth.

"A girl?" Mildred asked. "No" was the answer. "A boy?", and Missie barked three times.

Again the woman objected. "The doctor is quite certain it will be a girl."

But Mildred continued to pursue the details. "What time will the baby be born?" Missie barked nine times. "Nine o'clock in the morning?" "No" was the answer. "In the evening?", and Missie said yes.

"I'm afraid that's quite impossible," the lady-in-waiting exclaimed. "The doctor isn't in the hospital at night and he has scheduled the operation for nine o'clock in the morning."

"How much will the baby weigh?" Seven barks.

"Well, I doubt it," the woman said. "My other babies only weighed five pounds."

She took her leave, thanking the woman and her dog for their interest and stating that she was amazed at the dog's comprehension of the questions but she was quite sure the dog was wrong on all counts. Mildred asked that she call when the baby came.

On the night of September 28, Mildred received an excited phone call from the woman's husband. "My wife became quite ill this evening and had to be rushed to the hospital," he exclaimed. "Her doctor was out of town and so another doctor assisted. She gave natural birth to a baby boy at exactly nine P.M." "How much did the baby weigh?" Mildred asked. "Seven pounds, and the baby's fine!"

Once accepting the incredulous fact that a dog can be clairvoyant, one is faced with the question as to why it could be more accurate even than its human counterparts. One can only speculate that the universal source of information flows to human and dog seers alike, but perhaps the human rational mind gets in its own way, distorting the information, whereas the dog just passes it along in whatever way it can. Was all of this vast knowl-

edge of past, present, and future events stored somewhere within the terrier's cranium? Perhaps not, yet
somehow it was made available to Missie and she was
sufficiently in tune with this source that she could act as
a near-perfect channel.

But to one salesman, at least, Missie was a virtual
library. He came knocking on Mildred's door, wanting
to sell her a set of encyclopedias. "I have a walking one
right here," she replied. "What do you want to know?"
Once he adjusted himself to the situation and decided to
humor his potential buyer, the salesman settled on the
subject of the Civil War. He asked a number of questions. Unhesitantly the answers came back from the pint-
size genius in front of him. "I guess you're right, lady,"
he said, packing up his samples and shaking his head.

"Dogs can't reason, the scientists say, but Missie did."
We could hardly argue with our hostess at this point,
sitting mesmerized and just a little numb on our portion
of the sofa. Sissie, the dog, jumped up on my lap and
wanted to play. I looked into her eyes and for an instant
imagined myself peering through these windows into unknown worlds beyond. "She isn't psychic," her owner
had said. But I couldn't help wondering. I tossed the ball
she held in her mouth. She leaped from my lap in pursuit
and I experienced some comfort in that.

"Do you know that Missie always knew what time it
was," the voice next to me was saying. "I would say to
her, 'Missie, what time is it?' Without bothering to look
at the clock, Missie would bark out the hour closest at
hand. If I asked her if it was before or after the hour,
she would let me know and then bark out the minutes
involved."

"How did you train her to do that?"

"Oh, I didn't train her," Mildred said with an em-
phatic gesture of her hands. "She did it entirely on her
own, just like all the other things. A friend made a play
clock for her with hands that could be turned on the face.
Sometimes she would prance over to her clock and set
the hands where they belonged for the hour. A child

might move the hands in any direction, but Missie always moved the hands in a clockwise fashion.''

Mildred leaned back against the overstuffed sofa and sighed. ''But Missie was no saint. She wasn't perfect. In so many ways she was like a small child. It was strange that she could be so knowing, so wise, and yet be so childish . . . I say childish, for Missie behaved more like a spoiled child prodigy than a dog.

''She was a ham, always wanting center stage. She loved to show off for people. For that matter, she loved people, all kinds of people, including the truckers that would stop in the alley behind the house. She would stand at the window and throw them kisses by pursing her mouth and then sending it off with a paw. She really made an effort to kiss and not lick like other dogs.

''She could raise a fuss when she wanted something and didn't get it. I would carry her in a little sack when I went shopping and she would be quiet as a church-mouse until she spotted something she wanted, like a small stuffed toy, and particularly if it was pink. Everything had to be pink. Dogs are supposed to be color blind, but Missie wanted everything pink whether it was her toys, flowers, clothes, or her ice cream. But if she wanted something in a store and I didn't get it for her, she would go 'ooo-oo-OO' and kick at me. Twice she shoplifted, dropping something in my sack when I wasn't looking. Then she would deny that she had put it there.

''When visitors came, she would run and get her pig-gybank, place it in front of them, and then pound on the top of it for dimes. It had to be dimes because she knew that it took a dime to buy a pink ice-cream cone from the ice-cream man. If you tried to drop something else in, she would grab her bank and run away. When she got her ice cream, she wanted to hold the cone between her paws to eat it. If you put it in her dog pan, she wouldn't have anything to do with it. Even when she was a puppy, she wanted to hold her bottle with her paws. She always had a box of pink chocolates, and when she performed for someone they were expected to give her a chocolate and she wouldn't accept it from anyone else. On one occasion the veterinarian gave her a shot in her fanny, and, like people talking about their operations, Missie had to call everyone's attention to her wound by wiggling her fanny at them.''

Mildred thumbed through a scrapbook on her famous dog, and as her eyes focused on some item that recalled a particularly fond memory, we were forgotten for a moment. Then she glanced at us and smiled wistfully. "Missie was very conscious of schedules and routines. Everything had to be in its place. Before she went to bed at night—dressed in the pink pajamas that were to be put on her by my mother—the furniture had to be where it belonged. If someone had moved the coffee table, she would put her paws against it and, giving her 'ooo-oo' sound, try to shove it back in place.

"When she awakened in the mornings and before she got out of bed, she would kind of bow on her forepaws and produce a sound like 'aum-aum-aum,' as though she was chanting. Later we heard the 'aum' chant done by Hindus and it sounded almost identical to Missie's morning song. Every morning she had to have her beads put on. She would then go to the bathroom for her morning chore and then insist that we immediately dispose of the paper. This out of the way, she wanted her jacket put on and it was time for breakfast—buttered pancakes or toast. She would eat cereal, but she had to be spoonfed. No dog dishes, please.

"When she went to bed, it was imperative that a certain stuffed dog be there. Not just any toy would do, and that was her bed dog and it was to remain in the bed. She was very careful with all of her toys and, when a visiting dog chewed on one of her stuffed dogs, she took it to bed and nursed it. After she played with a toy, she put it up again.

"Each new day was an adventure for Missie and always exciting to me, for I never knew what she would do next. She loved to ride escalators and trains at the amusement park. But one ride was never enough. After the first ride she would raise a fuss, saying 'Huh-uh, huh-uh,' until you took her a second time, and then she was ready to get off. One day she saw a boy playing with a hoop and she ran home and got out her ring and tried to play with it as he had. There was always something, like the time she saw a mounted deer head in a store. She had me hold her up so she could kiss it and then kept trying to find the rest of the deer. Somebody gave her a hula skirt. I asked her, 'Do you know what a hula dance is?' She immediately responded, 'Uh-huh, uh-huh, woof, woof, woof,' for yes. She started dancing on her two hind legs—she often stood up this way—stomping her feet, and she whirled around so fast that the hula skirt waved in the wind and is blurred in this snapshot, as you can see. As far as I know, she had never seen a hula dance unless on television.''

As Missie's fame grew, her activities and achievements were witnessed by many people. Wisely, Mildred obtained many notarized affidavits and received many signed letters. One of these was written by Dennis Gallagher, a member of the Colorado house of representatives and now a state senator. He stated:

''To whom it may concern:

''One day in the spring of 1966, while visiting Miss Mildred Probert, her little Boston terrier, named My Wee Missie, gave quite a performance for me.

''To my amazement the little dog, when asked by Miss Probert, barked out correctly my social security number, my phone number and address and the number of letters in the street on which I live. She then gave the complete birth date; month and year.

''She responded without hesitation and Miss Probert gave her no clues of any sort. Miss Probert would not have known these numbered items mentioned above. I can only respond to all of this in much the same manner someone in Shakespeare's play, *Hamlet*, Act I, Scene V, says to Horatio: 'There are more things in heaven and earth, Horatio, than are dreamt of in your philosophy.' . . . Respectfully submitted . . .''

Among Missie's many predictions were the wide use of new medical drugs, the use of artificial hearts, and major breakthroughs in the causes and cure of cancer. She predicted the cost to the dollar of the cost of construction of a large educational building. She could tell what grades a student would receive on his report card and the channels that various television shows appeared on.

Only once did Missie predict a person's death, for Mildred discouraged this type of question. The single occasion is best told in the following letter:

"In February 1965, we visited our neighbor Mildred Probert. She had her little clairvoyant Boston terrier, My Wee Missie, answer some questions for us. She barked out the birth dates of our three daughters very plainly and easily understood. Missie also gave the number of letters in our names and the time of day and her own address, including the zip code number.

"Then my husband put the dog in a chair, leaned over her, and asked, 'How many months will I live?' Miss Probert protested. She did not want her dog to predict death, and cautioned little Missie not to answer that question.

"My husband insisted on the dog answering and would not release her. (He said he felt he would live only a few months—not years.) Missie answered his question with 'twenty-five.' Miss Probert quickly said, 'Perhaps she means twenty-five years.'

"He then asked the dog, 'How many years will I live?' Missie immediately answered 'two.' He continued, 'Could you tell me the date, the month?' Missie answered 'Four.' He asked, 'The day?' She replied, 'Three' '1967.'

"This event came true, exactly as the dog predicted. My husband, C. Kincaid, died on April 3, 1967. The fourth month, third day, twenty-five months (two years) later. All the members of our family saw Missie perform her gift of prophesying innumerable times." The letter was signed "Norma Kincaid Price."

Mr. Kincaid had told Mildred that his doctor had told him that he had terminal stomach cancer and would live no longer than three to five months. He had died of accidental gunshot wounds.

Death was predicted by Missie only one other time—her own.

One day in May 1966, a few days before her eleventh birthday, Missie kept calling Mildred's attention to the time, but she would bark eight o'clock. Since it was not that time, Mildred would ask her what time it said on the clock. Missie would then bark the correct time but would immediately go back to barking eight o'clock. She did this seven times that day, Mildred recalls. At exactly eight P.M. Missie died, choking on a piece of food. All efforts to save her were to no avail. Later, Mildred discovered Missie's toy clock in a corner of the room. The hands had been turned to eight o'clock.

Three weeks later, Missie, Mildred, and Missie's veterinarian would have been on their way to Hollywood, where Missie was to star in a Walt Disney film. All arrangements had been made, starting with a publicity banquet in Missie's honor in a large Los Angeles hotel. All decorations were to be done in pink.

"She never looked any older. To the day she died she appeared to be a puppy. Rigor mortis did not set in for thirty-six hours, until just before the autopsy. Our veterinarian had called the Colorado School of Veterinarian Medicine at Fort Collins to ask if they wanted Missie's brain because of its unusual brilliance. They stated they would be pleased to receive her brain."

Missie was buried in the backyard of the home. The pink petunias that she loved were planted on her grave, and though petunias are annuals that die with the first hard frost, these petunias continued to bloom through the winter, and the temperature dropped to seventeen degrees below zero. The grave—as shown by several of Mildred's snapshots—has continued to remain green all year.

Silence crept in on us, but there in the old Victorian

halls were the echoes of another day. "Ah, Mildred," Jeann'e said, "what a blessing to have experienced something so rare and so beautiful!"

I could only nod.

So many times since, my attention captured by a dog playing patiently with a small child in a park, I have looked up and seen my own dog studying my face, or perhaps when I have slipped into a philosophical mood in my den late at night, I have found myself thinking about Missie. She remains, of course, an enigma, for how can we offer plausible reasons for her behavior and achievements? We can only speculate.

It would seem that we are faced with one of two choices. Either we have completely underestimated the intelligence of dogs, along with considerable psychic skills, or Missie, in essence, was not a dog but a dog's body was simply serving as an earth vehicle for a higher intelligence.

If the former, it is thought-provoking to ponder the implications of future discoveries in animal behavior. If the latter, why would an advanced intelligence choose a canine body through which to incarnate? To deliver a message to humans concerning the value of other life forms on this planet? To humble us and force us to re-think our treatment of other creatures? Maybe one day we'll know.

Yes there is a bottom line to both arguments. Which-ever we choose, we are closer to the position that mind is something other than and not limited to the organic brain. Further, the capabilities of the mind are not lim-ited by the brain, nervous system, and body structure. Although the expressions of the mind may be restricted by lack of complex verbal expression, a thumb, opposite fingers, etc., behind the animal system may be an intel-ligence far superior to those levels we have assigned it.

CHAPTER FIVE

A Higher State

"Comparative psychologists have gone from wondering whether apes can comprehend symbols to detailing the ways in which they acquire and use them. Other scientists are documenting similar abilities in sea mammals. Still others are finding that birds can form abstract concepts. The news isn't just that animals can master many of the tasks experimenters design for them, however. There's a growing sense that many creatures—from free-ranging monkeys to domestic dogs—know things on their own that are as interesting as anything we can teach them."

Geoffrey Crowley, author of the above statement, explains in his article, "The Wisdom of Animals," in the May 23 issue of *Newsweek*, that the new research is raising questions about the human place in the scheme of things. He quotes Herbert Terrace, a psychologist at Columbia University as saying: "For thousands of years humans believed that they are the only creatures capable of thought." It has been tough on us to admit that we're physically descended from and related to other species. But the implication of the new research is that even our minds are part of an evolutionary continuum.

"Thinking, it turns out, is not a special power that sets us apart from the rest of nature but a biological adaptation we happen to share with much of the world," Geoffrey notes. "Animal-rights activists see a profound moral message in this. Scientists, by contrast, see the possibility of a deeper understanding of ourselves and the world. By exploring the nuances of other creatures' thought processes, we gain a new perspective on our own. We see how we're different, and how we're not. We see, in a sense, who we are.''

"We're not on a pedestal someplace, alone and magnificent," dolphin researcher Ken Norris states. "Dolphins are one branch of a tree we are all a part of. We are of them, they are of us, and the more we know about them and the other animals, the fewer the barriers there will be between us.''

Rolling Thunder, an Indian medicine man from Nevada, once told me: "How can man understand life if he is not part of it. He must learn to live in the heart of the coyote. This is not a poetic gesture of imagining what the wolf or the owl feels; the medicine man must direct his consciousness within the animal and understand himself as a bird, a coyote, and so on. He must actually see through the eyes of the coyote, hear through its ears, to think its thoughts . . .''

This amazing ability of the human to learn from animals about the world usually assumed to be beyond their level of understanding is not limited, of course, to any particular group of people. It is a state of awareness that can be gained by anyone who is patient enough to listen to life.

Boone tells of finding this quality in a man who spent his life in the desert in company with animals. He states in *Kinship with all Life* that Mojave Dan "was the only human I had ever personally known who could carry on silent two-way conversations with animals and really share ideas with them. Dan never reads books, magazines, or newspapers, never listens to the radio, never watches television and seldom asks questions of other humans, yet he is amazingly well informed at all times about practically everything that interests him, either nearby or afar. This information comes from his dogs and burros, from wild animals, from snakes, from insects, from birds, indeed from almost everything that crosses his trail. The real mystery was not so much Dan's ability silently to communicate his thoughts to the animal but his capacity to understand when the animal spoke to him.''

True understanding of life, according to Rolling Thunder, operates from a point within the mind itself, where there is understanding of oneness between what is Self and non-Self. This oneness assumes that nothing interposes between them. There is no memory, association, choice, or discursive thinking about the object. If one can experience such a thing in its nakedness, apart from any properties attributed to it, he can experience oneness with the object, and the subject-object arrangement loses its significance. The undifferentiated vision is what awakens one to spiritual awareness, the medicine man said. ''This awareness is out of space and time, it has passed beyond both.

''With one's mind, one can reach toward an object and discover an identity. But the identification does not need to be made, for it is experienced by the removal or stilling of that which intervenes between the two. Unity is experienced through being.''

And I can hear another Indian medicine man, Mad Bear of the Iroquois, saying that what we think of as consciousness is only the mental range of the human and that there is much that is invisible, inaudible, and intangible to most men. ''There are ranges of consciousness,'' he told me, ''that most people have no contact with, but unconsciousness is simply another level of consciousness. Unconsciousness does not exist in the universe. Consciousness can be found in the animal, the plant, the atom, in everything of nature. We are not fully awake if we do not experience consciousness in nature.''

It would seem that the more awake or enlightened the individual the more his realization that consciousness permeates life itself and not merely one of its forms. Ramakrishna, Pantanjali, Jesus, Buddha, Mohammed, Wesley, Schweitzer, Black Elk, Einstein are just a few of the world's greatest minds who could communicate and learn from all kinds of animals in addition to the human one.

"It is from understanding that the power comes; and the power in the ceremony was in understanding what is meant; for nothing can live well except in a manner that is suited to the way the sacred Power of the World lives and moves," Black Elk states in *Black Elk Speaks*, the classic by John G. Neihardt.

Black Elk has had a vision and he makes it clear that a man who has a vision is not able to use the power of it until after he has performed the vision on earth for the people to see. Part of the vision had to do with gaining the powers of the bison and the eagle and much was taken in designing a ritual that would manifest these powers. At one point in the ceremony, Fox Belly chanted the following words:

"A sacred herb-revealing it, they walk.
Revealing this, they walk.
The sacred life of bison—revealing it, they walk.
Revealing this, they walk.
A sacred eagle feather—revealing it, they walk.
Revealing this, they walk.
The eagle and the bison—like relatives they walk."

Don Juan, the Yaqui shaman, makes it quite clear to his student, Carlos Castaneda, that in order to understand the teachings, he must gain knowledge of the spirit inhabiting the body of the animal. "It was not a dog! How many times do I have to tell you that? This is the only way to understand it. It's the only way! It was 'he' who played with you," he insists in *The Teachings of Don Juan: A Yaqui Way of Knowledge*.

Many scientists are not speculating that brain and mind are not synonymous. Here they find themselves in agreement with mystics who have long claimed that the organic brain cannot be the sole component of mentality, that there is a nonphysical mind which uses the physical brain as an instrument. Within this model, the mind is not dependent on the brain for its existence. Actually, they say, the reverse is true: the mind creates and uses the brain in order to function within a physical body. If this model is accurate, the examination of the brain will fail to yield the nature, source, and degree of intelligence. The complexity of the brain—when fully understood—may provide us with some measure of insight as to how this control center operates a body capable of many activities.

Where all of this seems to be taking us is toward a conception of consciousness as not something produced by a body, nervous system, and brain but the other way around. A certain expression of consciousness creates a certain body, nervous system, and brain. We might venture that a particular kind of body system can contain or be the expression of a particular type of consciousness. However, it would seem that a study of the body system would provide us with an understanding of the nature of its consciousness only if we understand all of its various expressions. At this point we are still mapping and exploring our own consciousness, and it seems likely that our understanding of awareness other than our own is even less complete.

There is some evidence that part of the mind is in touch with everything in the universe, ignoring form, space, and time. Solving the riddles as to the nature of man and the other animals upon this planet may depend less on bisecting gray matter and mental guessing games and more in understanding the unified consciousness in which all life forms move and have their being.

"There is life on earth—one life, which embraces every animal and plant on the planet. Time has divided it up into several million parts, but each is an integral part of the whole. A rose is a rose, but it is also a robin and a rabbit. We are all part of one flesh, drawn from the same crucible," biologist Lyall Watson tells us in *Supernature*. "This is the secret of life. It means that there is a continuous communication not only between living things and their environment, but among all things living in the environment. An intricate web of interaction connects all life into one vast, self-maintaining system. Each part is related to every other part and we are all part of the whole.''

In some ways the mystery of animal behavior is considerably less than it was several years ago. A leading animal behavior researcher, Nikko Tinbergen, has stated: ''If one applies the term [ESP] to perception by a process not yet known to us, then extrasensory perception among living creatures may well occur widely. In fact, the echo-location of bats, the function of the lateral line in fishes, and the way electric fishes find their prey are all based on processes which we did not know about—and which were thus 'extrasensory' in the sense—only twenty-five years ago.''

Yet there are many kinds of animal behavior which clearly meet the definition of extrasensory perception— that is, the animal will be aware of events, conditions, etc., that cannot be traced to our present knowledge of the five senses. At this point there is little reason to believe that extrasensory perception in animals is different than it is in humans. It would seem safe to assume that when we learn more about extrasensory perception and psi (a Greek letter used generically for all types of psychic phenomena), our knowledge can be applied to both animal and human subjects. If, for example, we discover that awareness of consciousness is not something that is a product of the mechanical-chemical function of the body and not something limited by the space-time structure of the body, then the explanation of ESP may not reside in the body-organic brain-nervous system, but on other levels. In this case, the differences—if they exist— between animal and human paranormal abilities cannot be found merely by studying the differences in physical systems.

For laboratory tests, animals are usually placed in simple environments so that the environmental factors influencing the animal can be kept to a minimum. However, this approach fails to provide the investigator with a look at the natural behavior of the animal and undoubtedly this has an effect on the results. Nevertheless the results have been impressive.

Many of the studies provide the subject animal with a set of choices, one of which leads to an outcome desired by the animal. ESP is exhibited, it is believed, if the animal makes a sufficient number of right choices.

At Duke's parapsychology laboratory, Karlis Osis and Esther Foster ran a study on kittens placed in a T-shaped maze. The kittens were trained to understand that either arm of the maze could lead to concealed food. The food was then shifted around and the kittens had to decide which arm of the maze contained the food. Olfactory clues were minimized by blowing air away from the cats.

The kittens did well above chance when they were shown affection and when distractions were avoided. Fixed patterns, however, such as having the food on the right or left several times in a row, tended to discourage the animals' effectiveness.

Some studies have used a precognition procedure, in which the choice that will lead to the reward has not yet been made at the time that the animal chooses. C.E.M. Bestall and James Craig have found evidence that rats and mice placed in two-choice mazes are able to predict which of the two choices would later be designated randomly as the correct choice.

The most consistent and important set of animal studies, according to Robert L. Morris, Ph.D., research co-ordinator of the Psychical Research Foundation in Durham, North Carolina, are those initiated by Pierre Duval and Evelyn Montredon in France and continued in America by Walter Levy with gerbils and hamsters. The animal is placed in a small cage divided into halves by a partition which the animal can easily jump over. Once every minute or so, a mild shock is administered for approximately five seconds. A random-number generator electronically selects which side is shocked through the floor. The animal presumably is motivated to anticipate which side is about to be shocked so that it can jump on the nonshocked side. The animal's position is monitored electronically and the data is processed automatically. According to Dr. Morris, more than twenty successful series have been run using variations of the above procedures. There have been only a few failures.

In a similar study, Walter Levy found that lamps heating chicks and live chicken eggs in a cool environment also stayed on more often than would be expected by chance. This did not occur when the environment was heated sufficiently, nor did it happen when cooked instead of live eggs were used.

An interesting demonstration of canine ESP was conducted recently at Rockland State Hospital in Orangeburg, New Jersey. The experimenters built two copper-lined rooms that were vibration-proof and soundproof. In one of the tests, the owner of two hunting beagles was given an airgun and placed in a room where a slide projector showed pictures of animals he had actually hunted. He was to shoot the gun at the animals. Locked in the other room were the beagles, and they were viewed through a hidden observation panel.

When the hunter fired at a slide of a fierce wildcat, the beagles went wild with excitement even though they were in a separate soundproof and vibration-proof room apart from their owner. Their excitement continued as he fired at other animals on the slides, according to project director Dr. Aristide Esser.

In another experiment, a boxer was attached to an electrocardiograph in one room with his woman owner in a separate room. Without giving the woman any prior warning, a stranger burst into the room, shouting abuse at her and threatening physical violence. She was reportedly genuinely frightened, as can be imagined. Her dog in the other soundproof room must have sensed his owner was in danger, for at that very moment his heartbeat became violent.

On a recent trip to Denver I had to get some work done on my car. The mechanic noticed lying on the front seat several books on psychic phenomena and queried if I believed "in that kind of stuff." He quickly added that he certainly didn't put much stock in it himself. But my attempt to discuss some of the serious research in the field was soon interrupted by the man telling one incident after another about his big Labrador reading his mind and about a horse that always knew when to hide when some member of the family was thinking about riding.

There is a mountain of evidence supporting belief in the psychic power of animals—pets aware that their masters have died or are in danger although hundreds of miles away at the time; mind-reading feats; predictions of earthquakes, storms, and even bombings hours before they happen; the ability to traverse a continent in the search of a lost master; the returning from the dead to warn former owners of danger; even clairvoyance, as in the strange case of Missie, the Boston terrier whose story is told in the previous chapter. Strange tales of powers that few of us, the "superior" species on this planet, can demonstrate.

Several years ago, our next-door neighbor boarded a large Persian cat for her mother, who was visiting friends in England for the summer. The cat and the elderly woman had lived together in an apartment for four years and had not been separated for more than a day or two during that time. So it was understandable that the cat was upset for several days upon being left behind, but she soon adjusted to the new arrangement and seemed reasonably content. But a month after her mistress had left on the trip, the cat sat in a corner of the living room meowing piteously, refusing to eat, and ignoring all attention. Shortly after noon of the second day, the cat broke into a loud yowling. Within the hour, our neighbor received a telephone call that her mother had died en route to the hospital from a heart attack.

Perhaps animals make a greater effort to communicate with us than we realize and most of the messages never claim our attention.

Noted animal psychologist Beatrice Lydecker thinks

so. She has demonstrated on national television and to the satisfaction of a number of animal researchers her ability to communicate with animals. She sums up the results of her research in *What the Animals Tell Me*, stating that animals engage in nonverbal communication through ESP. Lydecker cites results of tests that demonstrate how a person can communicate with his pet using nonverbal language and visualizing what he wishes to communicate to the animal. Pet owners are advised as follows: ''To train the pet to understand the word 'sit,' for example, tell it to sit while you visualize it in that position. Soon the animal will respond to the command as it receives the image from you. While this instruction is going on, ESP communication is taking place. You are conversing in the animal's language. As you become more proficient, chatting with your pet (via ESP images) will seem natural.''

While such communication may prove difficult for many to believe, zoologists Maurice and Robert Burton observe in their new encyclopedia of animal behavior, *Inside the Animal World*, that ''it would take a lot to convince some dog owners that their animals do not communicate by telepathy.'' Their encyclopedia notes striking examples of animal telepathy. Finally, psychologist J. B. Rhine, noted for his research in this area, has reported that well-controlled experiments on ESP in animals confirm evidence suggesting that the ability of animals to send and receive telepathic messages is an acquisition of the animal organism that predates conscious senses.

Telepathy might explain the simultaneous change of direction of a flock of birds wheeling together in flight. It also might help us to understand how dogs and cats are able to track their owners over long distances to places they have never been.

Several years ago, researchers at the Institute for Parapsychology in North Carolina verified the story of a cat that traveled from New York to California to find its former owner. It seems that the owner, a veterinarian, gave his cat to friends when he moved across the country. Five months later, a cat arrived at the front entrance of his home. He was amazed how much the cat resembled his former pet and was further surprised when the animal entered the house and went directly to what had been his former cat's favorite chair. An examination of the cat erased any doubts, for it, too, had one vertebrae larger than the others.

Jack Millikan lived on a farm about twenty miles from Elgin, Illinois. One day he decided to take his Irish setter, Jessie, on a trip to the Rocky Mountains. However, near Lincoln, Nebraska, Millikan suddenly blacked out, his car ran off the road and was wrecked.

The next thing that Millikan remembers was waking up in the hospital. He immediately asked about his dog, but no one seemed to remember seeing a dog at the scene of the wreck. However, upon his release, Millikan started making inquiries and did locate a couple who remembered seeing a setter hanging around the wrecked car. But with no more leads as to the whereabouts of his pet, Millikan had to give up the search and returned to Illinois.

He left the farm and moved back to his parents' home in Elgin, a place that Jessie had visited a number of times. Six months after the accident, Millikan had left for work, but when his brother went outside, there in the yard was Jessie. The family decided that when the dog returned to the farm but could not find her owner, she headed to the home in Elgin, the only other place she associated with Millikan.

Newspapers for several years have reported on a young Brazilian youth, Francisco Duarte, who allegedly is able to communicate and give instructions to all kinds of animals and insects. Small for his size and considered mentally retarded, Duarte handles spiders, wasps, bees, snakes, frogs, rats, and alligators without being bitten or even attacked. Further, according to Alvaro Fernandes, a parapsychology investigator, all of the animals obey the instructions given to them by the youth.

According to the reports of Francisco and investigator Martha Barros, bees, for example, will land where Duarte tells them to and if he tells all of the bees to return to the hive except six, that is what happens. Poisonous snakes will coil, uncoil, or move to where he tells them, and fish will come to his hand in the water when he tells them to do so. Duarte told reporter Michael Joy, ''I talk to the animals and they talk to me. I can understand everything they say. My talent is a gift from God.''

As with any research, the study of animal intelligence has gone through its periods of belief and doubt. Several years ago, some scientists were doing a pretty good job of convincing the world that animal communication was little more than conditioned responses. But Duane and Sue Savage-Rumbaugh persevered in their studies at the Language Research Center, a joint venture of Yerkes and Georgia State University.

Working on the problem of symbolic representation, the Rumbaughs, with the help of two chimps, Sherman and Austin, have come a long way in dispelling any doubt that apes can really understand sign language. After having mastered pairing signs with objects, the chimps were able to learn tasks that would be impossible without the knowledge of the meaning of symbols. For example, Sherman and Austin were exposed to a screen on which was flashed a sign for an object. It was then necessary for one of the apes to go to a separate room stocked with many different objects and pictures and to return with whatever was flashed on the screen. Not only were the chimps able to retrieve the correct objects but would return empty-handed if that particular object was not in the room.

Following this achievement, Sherman and Austin have demonstrated that they not only understand the meaning of symbols but are able to communicate this information to one another. In one exercise, the chimps sit before a tray filled with food and place orders with one another.

At the University of California, Santa Cruz, Ron Schusterman has taught a thirteen-year-old sea lion by the name of Rocky to not only read hand gestures but to respond correctly to the gestures in sentencelike combinations she has never seen before. Trained at first to fetch different objects, Rocky then learned to decipher the difference, for example, in "Take the ball to the disc," and "Take the disc to the ball." To make sure that the sea lion is not just memorizing the phrases, Schusterman and his associates constantly hit Rocky with new combinations.

Crowley explained in the article mentioned earlier that pigeons are the undisputed masters of rote, and laboratory studies reveal that pigeons can memorize the contents of three hundred photographs, and possibly a great deal more. To see whether pigeons could graduate to open-ended categories, Richard Herrnstein, a Harvard psychologist, found that the birds could learn to look at photographs and select a member from a generic class, such as people or trees. "The birds not only mastered these categories, grouping oaks with pines and recognizing people regardless of age, sex, or color—they seemed in some trials to grope toward concepts, as when they succeeded at grouping raindrops with oceans," Crowley explained.

It has been discovered that the sonar or echolocating blasts of dolphins are actually short bursts of sound pulsing through the fatty tissue of the forehead, where they are focused into a beam that travels through the water several times faster than through the air, Justine Kaplan notes in his article, "The Day of the Dolphin," in a recent issue of *Omni*. This sound then bounces off a target and returns an echo that contains information on the surrounding environment. The dolphin hears through fat deposits in the jaw, from which the sound is transmitted to the inner ear and then to the brain. These broad bands of both low- and high-frequency sound emissions allow the dolphins to navigate in turbid waters and locate and identify objects well out of visual range, up to eight hundred meters away.

"There has been some speculation," Kaplan states,

"that dolphins may use their sonar to project images into other dolphins' brains. Perhaps sonar also gives dolphins an understanding of the humans that enter their environment. Pregnant women have reported that when they are in the water with dolphins, they can feel blasts of energy directed at their wombs. The echolocating beams are gentle, soothing vibrations that feel like energy pulsing through a machine."

Vicki Hearne—poet, English professor, and trainer of dogs and horses—points out that perhaps all animal gestures may convey information. Discussing Hearne's work, Crowley states that she argues with conviction that scientists, by focusing too narrowly on certain capabilities, often miss out on what's most interesting about their subjects. "How, she asks, can we presume to declare any particular ability—whether to juggle concepts or to communicate with symbols—a general measure of mental ability? 'We assume it's a homogenous phenomenon. There isn't just one kind of stuff that you can put in a bottle and call intelligence. When you define an animal's intelligence in terms of its ability to master a certain concept, you're projecting the concept into a new territory."

This serious limitation is touched on by Maurice Burton in his book *The Sixth Sense of Animals*. He states: "The more refined the techniques the narrower the field of vision, not only in the literal sense but in the sense that he is apt to forget that the tiny structure he is examining is only a minute part of the whole animal. So there is a divorce between what we know of the workings of the sense-organs and the use the animal makes of these organs in its everyday life. The gulf is not easy to bridge. It seldom, if ever, happens that a scientist skilled in the use of the electron microscope or microelectrodes has more than a passing knowledge of animal behavior, while the ethologist, the student of animal behavior, is aware of the finer laboratory researches to a limited degree only. We may go even further and say that the ethologist often derives his information from laboratory experiments or observation of animals in captivity, so that he may not be fully equipped to equate his results with what can be observed of the animal living free in the wild.''

And what happens when we peek behind the skull of the animal, when we divide it into little pieces? Can human and animal intelligence be meaningfully compared?

In order to determine the level of human intelligence, we measure a series of abilities. As different intelligence tests measure different abilities, the tests are impossible to compare. Because of this problem, human intelligence tests cannot be directly applied to other animals. Other animals live under different circumstances and therefore use quite different abilities.

These differences are pointed out by Vincent and Margaret Gaddis in their book *The Strange World of Animals and Pets*: ''Many wild animals become pathetic neurotics in captivity. In zoos they are deprived of the environments they require for normal behavior. They often react to monotony and frustration with violence; others suffer chronic depressions, sexual obsessions or inhibitions, and emotional ills that cause physical damage and even death.

''To attempt to make intelligence tests of wild creatures after they are imprisoned and their behavior patterns shattered, their senses torpid, and their minds sluggish, is ridiculous. Only in their natural habitat does their natural brilliance shine forth.''

The authors quote Ralph Helfer, Hollywood animal trainer, as saying that it is a mistake to believe that animals think in the same way that humans do. ''People mistakenly rate the intelligence of animals by their own,'' Helfer said. ''There is a wild intelligence in a tiger that is top rate, but which is different from our thinking.''

''Laboratory experiments seeking to determine animal intelligence use mazes or puzzle boxes, or have their subjects push or peck the right symbol to obtain a food reward,'' the Gaddises continue. ''These methods and similar ones are unsatisfactory, and at best may rate only the intelligence level and response time of the individual subject. For not only do the levels between various species vary, but there can be great difference between individuals within each species. There are smart cats and there are stupid cats. This explains why zoologists cannot agree on a specific intelligence scale."

The higher the intelligence of an animal the less he is guided by instinct and the more he must learn from his parents. To a large extent, he must be prepared to solve problems on his own. Such higher animals require a considerable period of time for learning and maturation. While it has been held that the human has the longest maturation period of any animal as regards mental faculties, it seems that the elephant takes equally long. Domesticated elephants are not considered mature enough to work until they are about twenty years old. And some believe that it takes the sperm whale longer than the human and elephant to mature.

In a *McCall*'s magazine article entitled "Animals Can't Think? Think Again," Dr. Michael Fox notes a number of attributes of animals. Under "insightful behavior," he notes that a dog will push a stool over to a low gate in order to climb over, and that a wild cat will tap the surface of a stream to imitate the movements of a fly in order to lure fish. Under "a sense of reciprocity," he states that a dog will solicit cheese from a table and when told "no," will go to the kitchen and return with a dog biscuit that will be placed in the owner's lap, all the while looking at the cheese. "Clearly, the offering is meant as an exchange."

Dr. Fox points out that animals have vivid imaginations and he states that a cat may pounce on or chase nonexistent prey. This, he states, "is clear evidence of imagination, another component of the ability to think." He also points to a "sense of humor" in animals, that animals can be playfully teased or mock-attacked without becoming aggressive or defensive, and "the shift in thinking necessary to interpret such behavior as nonserious requires a sense of humor—another sign of intelligence."

Perhaps Dr. E. D. Buckner, a physician who wrote extensively about animals at the turn of the century, was enough of a prophet to realize that someday research would come a long way in proving him right in what probably seemed to readers of his time unfounded proclamations. He stated in *The Immortality of Animals*, published in 1903:

"Hence animals are to be considered as creatures that move and act of themselves, or as having souls like man by which they are informed and directed. The memory of animals, their power of comparing, distinguishing, and reasoning, and, above all, their sense, which necessarily infers a sentient principle, are additional confirmations of this truth. . . ."

They are taught to converse in different languages, and answer in the same language in which they are addressed. Dogs and monkeys may be taught to use as many specific sounds and signs for specific things as some of the lowest types of man, which shows that they are capable of a progressive education. Many animals have the power of reasoning wonderfully developed. An elephant will break off a branch of a tree, grasp it in his trunk, and drive off the flies. He will blow beyond an object he cannot reach, and drive it toward him. When sick, he will go alone to a surgeon for treatment.

"Animals are progressive in the manner of receiving their education in all actions, the same as man. Take a puppy, for instance, and observe his gradual development, and the different mental stages of action, and you will notice he adds new thoughts and actions, and leaves many features of his early life behind when he grows older, just as we see in the gradual development of a child. Take a young canary bird, and you will observe that its first notes are imperfect, like a child learning to talk, but by a constant effort it will become proficient. Animals are slow and awkward. . . . As we observe the several faculties and traits of character, which belong alike to man and animals, we recognize that some knowledge of things is born with them and some acquired by a degree of education.

"It is by such phenomena of the animal soul that we

recognize its power of perception. The different kinds of perceptions are as numerous as the different channels through which they are received, and they are durable in proportion to the exciting cause. These impressions, as they are retained, become ideas. The mind has the power of suffering such ideas to remain latent or unobserved, and of calling them into observation at its option; and it is the active exercise of this power that constitutes thought. Reason is founded in the consciousness of thoughts by which actions are governed, and is the internal evidence of conscious thoughts and the power to arrive at a conclusion. To be governed by reason or abstract ideas is a general law imposed by the Creator upon all animals. An orangutan, in Paris, when left alone, tried to escape; and as he could not reach the lock of his door, he carried a stool to the spot, and mounting upon it, took his master's keys and tried each one until finding the right one, he unlocked the door as he had seen his master do, and walked out. Reason only could have prompted this act, as it would require a combination of ideas to perform it.

"The intelligence of lower animals is a profound mystery to us. We do not know what they think, nor the extent of their thoughts, but I am positive they have much more intelligence than is usually attributed to them, and that the germ of every human faculty exists in some form and in some species of animals. As one man does not possess all the faculties which the mind is capable of possessing, so it is with the faculty of any one of the lower animals, but in the aggregate they possess every incipient principle of every known faculty in man."

The ancient writer Pliny said that it was a shame that all animals knew what was healthful for themselves except man. He added that animals perform not only what might be termed as simple actions caused by necessity but complex actions where choice can only come from reason.

The Reverend John Wesley, founder of the Methodist Church around 1730, stated in reference to Adam: "God gave him such life as other animals enjoy,'' and ''Yea, they have all one breath so that a man hath no preeminence above a beast.''

And the eighteenth-century English scholar Sir Benjamin Brodie noted: ''The mental principle in animals is of the same essence as that of human beings.''

Throughout *Kinship With All Life*, J. Allen Boone stressed the need of the human being to recognize that real communication and rapport with animals depended largely upon respect for their intelligence and feelings. Without this acceptance, he explained, animals might be trained to obey human commands but there could be no real sharing.

There are some other implications that can be drawn. The evidence on hand would seem to indicate that there is an awareness beyond the so-called normal senses. This awareness puts the subject not only in contact with his immediate environment but also with things and events at some distance. This awareness may be shared not only by humans and animals but by all living things. If this should happen to be the case, then life, regardless of the form it takes, would seem to be enveloped by a universal and unifying consciousness. Each thing would be related to everything else, and each life form would to some minute degree affect and influence everything in the universe.

Perhaps one of the reasons we do not do better with nonverbal communication is that we keep our brains so busy computing data from our five senses that we pay little attention to the worlds of information reaching our supersenses. Animals, less belabored by the complexities of life, are more in tune with nature and the psychic dimensions than ourselves.

Naturalist John Burroughs called it the hidden heart of nature, and some Indians refer to it as deep-knowing. Carl G. Jung described an intelligence beyond individual intellect, the great collective unconscious, the depository of all memories, thought, and knowledge, spaceless and timeless. This mental reservoir is the same everywhere, and all forms of life partake of and are enveloped within it. Living together within this Universal Being, individual minds, regardless of the physical form they seem to inhabit, become aware of each other in a new medium and share in ways never experienced before.

CHAPTER SIX

Prophets

She predicted to the day that the United States would enter World War II. She prophesied that Harry Truman would be reelected when no one but herself and Truman believed it, and she startled police by leading them to the body of a boy who had been missing for two years. This seer with a long history of accurate prophetic vision happened to be a horse—Lady Wonder—and she managed to pass J. B. Rhine's tough extrasensory examinations at Duke University parapsychology laboratory when many so-called accomplished two-footed psychics failed.

While Lady Wonders might not be found in many stables, nor Missies discovered in many households, animals of every type—footed, feathered, and finned—have long confounded man in their abilities to foresee events before they happen. Nowhere is this more in evidence than in the fields of weather and earth disturbances. Stories are legend of how animals are precognitive of storms, earthquakes, and other natural disasters, warning less sensitive humans hours, sometimes days, before the occurrences.

"Many animals seem to possess an extrasensory perception band that contributes to individual survival. Huge herds of cattle were grazing along the coast of Peru shortly before a major earthquake disaster in which a considerable length of the coastline actually fell into the ocean. When the earthquake occurred, there was not one animal in the endangered area," explained Manly Palmer Hall, president of the Philosophical Research Society, Inc., Los Angeles.

Three hours before an earthquake jolted northeastern Italy on May 6, 1976, pet cats suddenly left their homes and headed for open ground. A few hours before the 1964 Alaskan earthquake, cattle grazing in lowlands on Kodiak Island suddenly fled for high ground. Shortly before this earthquake occurred, animals in zoos as far away as Seattle reportedly behaved in an agitated fashion. Before shocks hit Chile and Peru, it was noticed that the sea gulls abandoned the shoreline to fly many miles out to sea.

Two to three hours before the first tremor of a recent earthquake hit the Fruili region of Italy, mice and rats left their hiding places, cats fled their homes, and dogs throughout the region barked incessantly fifteen to twenty minutes before the quake struck. The dogs refused to enter houses when beckoned by their owners. It was recorded that dogs barked continuously before the great San Francisco earthquake, and a few minutes before the quake, horses and cows snorted and stampeded.

The August 26, 1963, issue of the Denver *Post* quoted Dr. Edgar W. Spencer, of Washington and Lee University, as stating that prior to the 1963 earthquake in southeastern Montana, birds disappeared from the major quake area several hours before the first tremor was felt.

The March 24, 1969, *U.P.I. Report on Soviet Studies* reported that a Russian woman living in Tashkent claimed that her spitz dog saved her life in the Soviet earthquake of 1966. The dog dragged her outdoors and away from the house just a few minutes before the quake destroyed her home. A Tashkent schoolteacher said that ants picked up their pupae and migrated from the anthills about an hour before the first shock. At the Tashkent Zoo the mountain goats and antelopes refused to enter their indoor pens quite some period before the quake, and days before the shock the tigers and other large cats started sleeping in the open.

Biologist Lyall Watson states in *Supernature*: "The Japanese, who live right on a fracture system, have always kept goldfish for this reason. When the fish begin to swim about in a frantic way, the owners rush out of doors in time to escape being trapped by falling masonry. The fish have the advantage of living in a medium that conducts vibrations well, but even animals living in the air are able to pick up warning signals. Hours before an earthquake, rabbits and deer have been seen running in terror from the epicenter zones. . . ."

Animal sensitivity is one of the components in a current push by the People's Republic of China to establish an earthquake prediction system. According to Dale Mead, writing in the March 1976 issue of *Science Digest*, a group of ten U.S. geologists and geophysicists recently visited China under the auspices of the National Academy of Sciences' Committee for Scholarly Communication with the People's Republic of China in order to learn more about their methods for predicting quakes. They learned that the Chinese were using electronic equipment, monitoring sounds coming from the earth and fluctuating water levels, and observing the strange behavior of animals.

China averages six quakes of at least 6.0 on the Richter scale each year, the highest in the world. Chinese methods of prediction have been so accurate, the visiting scientists reported, that they claim to have saved thousands of lives.

Mead stated in his article that the Chinese people were alerted to earthquake prediction methods employed by past generations. "The historical records said that farmers could tell that something was vastly wrong in the earth beneath them when normally placid horses reared and raced. Dogs howled. Fish leaped. Animals that were rarely seen, like snakes and rats, suddenly surged from their hiding places by the dozens. . . ."

To test the Chinese animal-watching techniques in this country, Dr. Barry Raleigh, of the U.S. Geological Survey's earthquake research facility at Menlo Park, California, visited Hollister County in California, a rural area prone to smaller quakes. He and a colleague, Dr. Jack Everndon, asked farmers and ranchers in the area if they had noticed animals behaving strangely before the November 1974 jolt. While a number questioned had not thought of observing animals, one woman told the scientists, according to Mead, that she had tried to calm two horses that were quite spooked for reasons then unknown. A colt ran around in such a frenzy, she said, that it fell down. Everndon discovered that the ranch stood almost directly over the center of the quake.

Dr. Everndon was told by a San Fernando official that two police units in separate areas reported seeing large numbers of rats scurrying in gutters the night before a major quake in 1971.

Until recently, scientists have dismissed the notion that animals were aware of pending earthquakes. But as observations about strange animal behavior become collected from all over the world, coupled with new scientific information about the sensory abilities of animals, more and more scientists began to take a closer look at the reports. These have been buttressed by some recent experiments testing animals in earthquake situations.

Dr. John M. Logan, working in earthquake research at the Center for Tectonophysics at Texas A & M University, comments that "all this reinforcement suggests that something is there.

"As a matter of fact," Dr. Logan says, "documentation in China is very good. The Chinese already use animals as an aid in prediction. A document distributed to the populace by the government of the People's Republic of China tells what to watch for.

"Reports on animal behavior from such diverse areas as Japan, the U.S., Italy, and Guatemala are similar, and such common observations come from people who could not possibly have had contact with each other or have read reports from other areas. This provides credibility to their reports and presents a large body of evidence supporting the contention that animals do sense something before earthquakes.

"A second point is that the response of the biological community is not restricted to a simple species or genus, but spans a very wide spectrum of biological forms. This suggests that either more than one stimulus, or a major universal one, must be detectable by a great variety of organisms.

"Most of the animal reports can be classified as startle-responses. It is generally concluded that such responses, when associated with earthquakes, are probably not learned. Stimuli-producing variations in animal behavior may simply exceed some noise level." As to how a quake-prediction program using animal behavior would be formulated, he indicates two probable forms:

Either recognition of variation in animal behavior preceding earthquakes (which would satisfy the immediate need of a predictive tool even if the mechanics of the process are not understood); or discovery of what stimulates the animals and monitoring of that physical signal without the intermediate step of observing animals' behavior.

Dr. Evernden says: "We would be remiss if we did not make some effort to build up scientific evidence to confirm or reject theories about animal behavior and quake prediction."

Dr. Evernden outlines several possibilities that might explain quake-sensing abilities. One hypothesis is that certain animals, sensitive to small variations in the earth's magnetic field, may sense a change in the field before the earthquake. It is possible that electrostatic charges in the air may be sensed by animals (and may also explain the phenomena of "earthquake lights").

Animals may sense properties of rocks that change as stress builds up before an earthquake, but what these properties are is not yet clear. Other physical phenomena could be sensed; for example, birds can detect magnetic variations, polarized light, ultraviolet light, very small changes in barometric pressure, and infrasound.

"It is easy and simple to use animals to predict earthquakes," states a booklet from the Seismological Office of Tientsin, China. "Certainly organs of animals may acutely detect various underground changes. Both historical and recent surveys prove that animals have precursory reactions." The booklet then provides these clues, in verse form:

"Animals were aware of precursors before earthquakes;
Let us summarize their anomalous behavior for prediction.
Cattle, sheep, mules, and horses do not enter corrals,
Rats move their homes and flee.
Hibernating snakes leave their burrows early.
Frightened pigeons continuously fly and do not return to nests.
Rabbits raise their ears, jump aimlessly, and bump things,
Fish are frightened, jump above water surface.
Every family and every household joins in observation.
The people's war against earthquakes must be won."

An earthquake destroyed more than three-fourths of Skopje, Yugoslavia, on July 26, 1963. It was reported that during the early-morning hours of that day, the animals of the local zoo aroused the zookeepers from their sleep. Elephants charged the bars of their cages, tigers and other cats paced their cages and constantly roared, and two bloodhounds at the police station leaped at the windows in efforts to escape the building. Officers on patrol particularly noticed the absence of birds in the town.

Naturalist Ivan Sanderson contends that what is involved in animal prediction of earthquakes is more likely supersensory perception than what we usually think of as extrasensory perception. Referring to Sanderson's theories, Vincent and Margaret Gaddis state in *The Strange World of Animals and Pets*: "Such acute awareness may detect approaching hurricanes by water-level fluctuations or drops in barometric pressure. Slight sounds or a rise in temperature may herald avalanches. Volcanic eruptions and earthquakes may be preceded by greater tensions in the earth's magnetic field. Animals may respond to minor trembling and small foreshocks.''

Sanderson once watched fiddler crabs by the thousands march inland from the coast of Honduras ahead of a hurricane. The march started twenty-four hours ahead of the storm. The coastal area was badly flooded but the fiddler crabs knew exactly how far to move inland to avoid the dangerous effects of the tidal wave.

The Bezymyanny volcano struck the Soviet Union during the winter of 1955–1956 but not a single bear was killed even though many lived in the vicinity of the volcano. According to Russian scientists, the bears interrupted their hibernation and found safer spots to await spring several days before the volcano's activity was first noted on instruments.

Nandor Fodor states in his *Encyclopedia of Psychic Science* that prior to the eruption of Martinique's Mount Pelee in 1902, the cattle became extremely restless and could not be managed, dogs howled continuously, snakes left the vicinity, and birds stopped singing and left the area.

The swift has long been respected as a weather prophet. Sometimes called the storm-swallow, rain-swallow, and thunderbird as a consequence of its successes, the bird has been known to predict storms by evacuating an area when the storm is more than eight hundred miles away.

A farm family living near Lawrence, Kansas, had a cat that predicted a tornado. The cat gave birth to four kittens in the barn. A few days later, however, the family noticed that one of the kittens was missing, and on subsequent days, another kitten was discovered to be missing, until all of the kittens were gone from the barn. That night after the last kitten disappeared, a tornado completely wiped out the barn. The mother cat and her kittens were reported to be safe and sound at a neighbor's house a few miles away. This place had not been touched by the storm.

Mrs. Freda Robinson of Oklahoma City watches her tomcat Felix rather than the local television stations for an accurate prediction of the weather. For four years now Felix always takes refuge in the top of the Robinson wardrobe when the weather is going to turn wet and stormy. On the other hand, if he settles down on the windowsill, sunny skies can be expected. Mrs. Robinson claims that Felix has never been wrong.

It is claimed that snakes in a zoo will invariably hide from human beings when rain is forthcoming. However, the traditional long-range weather forecaster is the groundhog. It seems that the groundhog always emerges from its place of hibernation on the same day each year— February 2. If the day is cloudy and he cannot see his shadow, then he will remain in the open. This allegedly means that the weather will be mild for the remainder of the winter. But if he pops back into his hole, don't pack your thermies—six weeks of frosty weather remain.

Gene Hereth of the U.S. Animal Research Trust has studied the results of groundhog forecasting for the past eighteen years and states that the creature has been accurate fifteen out of eighteen times.

Animals have not only been successful in precognitive monitoring of the weather and natural catastrophes but they have done well in foretelling imminent danger from man-made storms as well.

When England was being pounded almost nightly by the German Luftwaffe during World War II, many Englishmen learned to watch their cats for a signal that a bombing raid was forthcoming.

Before the approaching bombers were picked up on radar and the alert was sounded, cats were noticed to spring into action. The hair would stand up on their backs and they would race for the bomb shelters. Humans soon learned to quickly follow. Stories ran in the English newspapers, and before the war ended, the cats were awarded the Dickin Medal, engraved with the words "We Also Serve."

An explosion of a different sort apparently was predicted by a cat that enjoyed sleeping on or beside a television set. Vesey-Fitzgerald, writing in the British *News of the World*, told of the cat, who belonged to a friend. One day the cat jumped off the set, stared at it intently for a few seconds, and then demanded to be let outdoors. Thereafter, whenever the set was on, the cat would leave the room. Several days later, the picture tube exploded, blowing fragments of glass about the room.

In 1956, Ted and Dorothy Friend told in their column in the San Francisco *Call-Bulletin* of a woman with the unusual name of Welcome Lewis who was saved by the psychic premonition of her boxer. Mrs. Lewis brought her dog with her from Los Angeles while visiting in San Francisco. She took him to Lafayette Park for exercise, but the boxer refused to get out of the car. Instead, he barked and raised quite a fuss. Finally, Mrs. Lewis gave up and returned to her hotel. The dog did not hesitate to leave the car.

The following day she passed the same park and discovered that a huge tree had fallen on a car in the exact place where she had parked. She also learned that the tree had fallen only minutes after she had pulled away.

A heartwarming story of a dog protecting a woman he did not know is told by Louise Rucks in her April 24, 1976, column "Hound Hill," which runs in the *Oklahoman* and *Times*. It seems evident that the animal could foresee danger for the woman and therefore took steps to protect her. Mrs. Rucks quotes the letter:

"I enjoy your Hound Hill, and look forward to it every week. My main reason for writing you is to tell you of a queer experience I had with a large black dog while I was in Baltimore five years ago when my husband was in the Marine hospital and had leukemia. This is a true story and actually happened to me.

"At that time there were many rapes and muggings going on in daylight as at night. My husband and I worried about my walking the three dark blocks from my rented room to the hospital.

"The second night this huge solid black dog stepped out of a hedge and all but scared me to death. He walked me to the hospital and waited until I went back to my room. He stayed down on the sidewalk, never taking his eyes off me, until I climbed the steps and opened the door to the house. I was in Baltimore for two weeks and each night that wonderful dog escorted me to and from the hospital and waited to see me safely in the house. How safe and relieved I felt!

"The last time I saw him was the day I had to leave for home. He escorted me to the hospital and back but did not show up that night as my husband was released and walked with me. I do not know where the dog came from or where he went nor how he knew I would not need him the night my husband was released. I do not know how or why he knew I needed him.

"I have wanted to tell you this for a long time. Ever since I found your Hound Hill in the *Oklahoman*. But it sounded so weird. I hesitated until I could stand it no more."

And Mrs. Rucks comments: "This letter didn't sound weird to me. I agree with Henry Beston, nature writer, who wrote that animals are not brethren or underlings. They are 'other nations, caught with ourselves in the net of life and time, fellow prisoners of the splendor and travail of the earth.' Fellow nations do sometimes come to another's aid."

Spotty, a dog of mixed blood but mostly German shepherd, also had a premonition that his presence was required to protect a woman from danger.

The July 1959 issue of *Fate* related that during the Depression years of the 1930's, Mrs. Maude S. Translin of Palo Alto, California, was working at Stanford University. Near her home was a hobo jungle, and it bothered her that she was alone until late at night. Then Spotty was given to her by a friend who was a policeman. The dog was intelligent and he understood that he was to serve as watchdog for his mistress after dark. During the day, however, he was allowed to go with her son to his job.

One summer afternoon, Mrs. Translin arrived home from the university around five and was surprised to find Spotty waiting for her on the porch. This was the only time he had ever done this. Spotty entered the house and planted himself so that he could watch all entrances.

Mrs. Translin opened the house, including the doors, in order to cool it off and went into the bedroom to change clothes. Shortly she heard a loud rap at the front door. Frightened but not knowing what else to do, she called out, "I'll be right there." A rough man's voice growled an agreement. The next sound she heard was Spotty's toenails clicking across the floor and the man's voice calling out, "Will this dog bite?"

"Indeed he will! Just stand still," she responded. When Mrs. Translin emerged from her bedroom, she found Spotty standing at the front door, his throat rumbling and his teeth bared.

Her knees shook as she took hold of Spotty's collar. The caller was a huge, mean-looking man who snarled, "I'm hungry and I want a meal."

"I can't let go of the dog, but if you will shut the door and wait, I'll bring you something out in the yard."

The task was completed and the man left. Mrs. Translin sank to her knees and threw her arms around Spotty's neck. He had walked several miles through the heat to be with her several hours before her son would have driven him home in the car. This was the only time he had come home in the three years they had owned him.

The Gaddises tell the story of William H. Montgomery, who decided to fish for flounder off the coast of New England. He prepared his boat and then whistled for his setter Redsy. Always, since puppyhood, Redsy jumped at the invitation to go fishing.

But this day she refused to come aboard. Instead, she stood on the dock and barked despite Montgomery's entreaties and sharp commands. There was no logical reason to believe that anything was wrong with the boat, and the weather that day was perfect, hardly a breeze and no clouds in the sky. More than fifty boats could be seen heading for the flounder banks.

Fortunately for Montgomery, he trusted the intuition of his dog. He knew something had to be wrong, and if his setter wouldn't go with him, then he knew it was best to stay at the dock. Many of the boats that went out that afternoon never returned. Within an hour of the time that Montgomery planned to set out, the wind rose to a tremendous gale and an unexpected storm moved in from the sea. Huge waves, some forty feet in height, hammered boats and coastal cottages to kindling wood. More than six hundred lives were lost in the storm. It was the great hurricane of 1938.

The year-and-a-half-long drought that plagued the Midwest during 1988 and the first half of 1989 was broken in Kansas by a series of heavy downpours that filled farm ponds and dried streambeds to overflowing. Evacuation was necessary in some low-lying areas, roads were closed, and a number of old bridges were swept downstream. Carter Paige of rural Wichita was visiting a farmer friend south of Augusta, Kansas, when one of the cloudbursts occurred. When the rain subsided some, Paige decided he would try to get back the twenty miles to his home. Riding with him in his pickup was his German shepherd, Duke. Five miles from the friend's house, Duke suddenly started vehemently pawing Paige, whining and finally barking, something he had never done before. Paige trusted his companion of seven years and knew that something was wrong. He stopped the pickup and the dog quieted down, but when he started moving the pickup forward again, the dog once again became highly agitated. Paige once again stopped the pickup. Although it was dark and a light rain still falling, Paige decided to investigate the road ahead with his flashlight. The dog insisted on accompanying him. Not a hundred yards ahead they discovered that the township bridge had been totally destroyed by the torrent which had been a quiet stream when they had passed over it only three hours before.

Rats traditionally abandon a vessel at the dock before the ship sinks at sea. Such stories are supported by the experience of actor Raymond Massey and his wife. They told the story to Broadway columnist Danton Walker, who reported it in his book *Spooks Deluxe: Some Excursions into the Supernatural*.

At one time, the Masseys had purchased a town house in Manhattan's East Eighties. Across the street was a large brownstone mansion that was then unoccupied but later leased by a socially prominent woman and her family. She told the Masseys she could not get rid of the hordes of mice that inhabited the building.

A few days later, Mrs. Massey was astonished to witness a mass exodus of mice pouring from the brownstone house. The small creatures appeared panicky and confused. When a number of them scurried toward the Massey residence, Mrs. Massey called the exterminator. Several days later the socialite committed suicide.

The mansion stood empty for a time but was finally sold to a wealthy playboy. His death made front-page news, but before it did, Mrs. Massey once again saw the mice leave the brownstone house in droves.

The next owner of the house was a prominent businessman. One morning while watering her plants in a windowbox, Mrs. Massey again witnessed the mice horde as it issued from the house across the street. A few days later the businessman, while flying his own plane, crashed in the Hudson River and drowned before he could be reached by rescuers.

Many stories are told of dogs predicting the impending death of their owners or someone close to them. A number of psychics allegedly predicted the assassination of Lincoln, but none more clearly than the President's dog.

The White House staff made every kind of unsuccessful attempt to quiet the dog when he suddenly went berserk. Although always so quiet and docile, shortly before the tragedy the animal raced around the house in a frenzy and kept up a dirge of unholy howling.

Thomas Hardy, the English novelist, had a wire-haired terrier as a close companion for thirteen years. The dog, named Wessex, showed a great liking for one of Hardy's friends, William Watkins. On a spring evening Watkins visited the Hardy home and Wessex rushed to meet him with excited barks. On this occasion, however, his excitement gave way to a piteous whine. Hardy thought that he had developed a sudden pain but investigation revealed nothing to be amiss.

Wessex joined Hardy and Watkins in the study. During the course of the evening, the terrier touched Watkins's sleeve with his paw several times and withdrew it with cries of distress. When Watkins left the Hardy home, he was in good spirits and seemed to be feeling fine.

Early the following morning the telephone rang. Wessex had a habit of barking when this happened, but this time he remained silent. He lay on the floor with his nose between his paws. Watkins's son was calling to say that his father had died suddenly about an hour after leaving the Hardy home.

An ancient proverb states: "Know a grain of sand completely and you know the universe in its entirety."

It is enough of a struggle to allow that some observant souls among us can know what is happening a thousand miles away or what tomorrow will bring. But when other creatures than ourselves perform these feats, it challenges our belief systems if not our sanity. We can cope with this information in one of several ways.

We can deny the validity of such reports, which is easiest because no further demands will be made upon our conceptual structures or ideologies. A few doors are closed to us after that, but then we can always keep company with those who enjoy dogma more than truth.

We can allow that maybe such things do happen, but, if so, that they are one of those mysteries we are sometimes confronted with, and since there is no way of understanding them, the best thing for us to do is shake our heads at the wonder of it all and then turn on the TV set to something that won't put too much of a strain on our cerebrum.

We can allow that at least some animals have psychic sensitivity and can foresee the future, and can decide that the answers to such phenomena must reside in a more thorough examination of all kinds of nervous systems and brains. A courageous gesture, perhaps, and one entirely acceptable within scientific traditions, but one that may prove disappointing. Within contemporary synergistic views, the whole is more than the sum of its parts. Adding up the contributions made by each part of a system fails to provide us with a picture of how the whole behaves with its parts intact. One of the problems with most laboratory explorations is that the researcher manipulates the subject while expecting the subject to behave in its normal fashion. No experimenter can divorce his feelings and thoughts from his project, and these provide a non-measurable input. According to the latest findings in physics, feelings and thoughts produce energy and the experimenter becomes an unconscious part of the circuitry.

If we seek to understand how animals, or some animals at least, can be prophets, some help may be forthcoming through greater in-depth investigation of animals' supersenses. It has been learned that many creatures are more sensitive than humans to subtle energy fields and vibrations. Because of this, they may pick up very slight variations in the environment and somehow recognize these as indicative of change. They react to these impending changes and we translate their behavior as prophecy. It would seem that the more civilized a people become the more they rely on technology to protect their survival and provide them with the things they want. For example, we no longer have to be sensitive to weather changes, for the local meteorologist will do this for us. The ability to distinguish between faint odors and slight sounds contributes very little to our survival.

Yet man can reclaim the awareness of his senses when

the occasion demands it. Writer Jim Phelan, who spent
fourteen years in prison, wrote:

"The tyro in jail has not only to learn a new language
and become adept in minor trickeries. He has to develop
new senses, become animal-keen in a thousand ways not
known to civilization. Long before the end of my second
year I could tell one warder from another, in the dark
and at a distance, by his breathing, by his scent, even by
the tiny crackings of his joint. Presently I could smell a
cigarette in another man's pocket six feet away, hear a
lip-still mutter in church even while a trained warder
missed every sound. From the way an official clears his
throat, a long-term prisoner will know whether that man
is likely to report him for smoking an hour later—a long-
sentence convict is not a person, he is an alert, efficient,
and predatory animal."

Many of the instruments we have come to rely on tell
us of a universe all around us of which we are unaware
without the assistance of the machine. Perhaps our fellow
creatures, who have as yet failed to develop their own
technology, are more aware of the worlds superimposed
on each other.

But better eyesight, hearing, alert responses, etc., do
not alone explain the nature of clairvoyance in people.
Nor does the superior sensitivity of animals explain how
a dog could know that his master was going to be assas-
sinated, how mice could foresee the death a number of
miles away of the owner of the property they were inhabiting, or how a dog would know to return to his house
on a particular occasion in order to protect his mistress.
Apparently something more than acute sensitivity is involved in such cases.

In an earlier chapter we discussed models of consciousness. If we can believe the new physics when it tells
us that physical forms can be traced to energy fields and
energy fields, in turn, disappear into consciousness, then
the world is a thought. Its entire existence can be found
in that which thinks it. All forms, all animals, and ourselves included, in the final analysis exist as a thought.

We have long believed that the ability to be conscious depended upon a certain structure and that the nature of this structure determined the degree of awareness. But the new physics tells us that the thought creates the form rather than the other way around.

This possibility offers us a different theoretical approach: The form or structure of a living unit may not always determine the extent or level of its consciousness. If, as the mystics have long contended, the brain is merely a piece of equipment used by the mind, then the mind may be aware, but if the brain is limited in its functions, then this awareness is inhibited—according to our standards—in its expression. Animals may in some ways be closer to the Universal Mind because they are not occupied so intently with the activities of the brain. They well may be projecting at all times a reflection of Universal Consciousness, in which time and space do not exist, but we, because of our own limitations, fail to compute it.

Space and time do not exist, we are told, in clairvoyant visions. These highly talented persons tell us that their perceptions are not a product of the rational mind but of the intuitive mind. Because of this, their insights are difficult to translate to those relying principally upon logic and language. Perhaps this is not dissimilar to the problems faced by creatures other than ourselves.

As Hall explained in *The Inner Lives of Minerals, Plants, and Animals*: "We can get to know something about animal mentation—we learn about their little conspiracies, we discover that they have certain types of memory and show real genius in getting what they want. Like human beings, they enjoy being spoiled and have a subtle manner of working their way into the affections of those around them. Even though the animal is not a complete mystery, we still wonder what it thinks about. Does it have an inner life beyond our understanding? Is it a good citizen of a world we have never been able to penetrate?"

CHAPTER SEVEN

Ghost Animals

A friend has a small log cabin away from it all in the high country of western Colorado. He uses the cabin several weeks during the summer months to put the finishing touches on whatever novel he happens to be working on at the time. The trail to his cabin is passable only by four-wheel-drive vehicles, but in years gone by there was a road used by miners, and later it served a logging operation.

One night while at the cabin alone he decided to wander through the nearby woods, as a full moon had cast a magic spell upon the tall and silent mountains. He was mesmerized by the breathtaking beauty surrounding him and thoughts of how fortunate he was to be there instead of in the city passed lazily through his mind. But he was jarred from his reverie by the distinct sound of horses' hooves pounding down the path toward him.

Not sure who might be horseback riding in those remote parts and at that hour of the night, he quickly stepped off the path and behind a large tree. The pounding of the hooves became louder, then they seemed to be directly in front of him, and then they slowly faded away down the trail.

He stepped from his hiding place, from which he had been able to see up and down the trail, and he was quite bewildered, for the horse was never seen. "The moonlight was so bright that one could even see the color of the grass," he told me, "and there was no way I could have missed seeing the horse as it passed . . . yet there was only the sound."

He heard the horse another time, about the same hour and on the same kind of night, but on this occasion he was too far from the trail to have seen the horse in any case. But one morning while a friend was visiting he asked, "Does someone around here ride a horse on the trail?"

A little startled, he mumbled, "Well, I don't really know . . . I suppose riders do come up this way once in a while . . . Why?"

"I suppose I'm not used to the peace and silence of this place. I woke up last night and couldn't get back to sleep so I pulled on my boots and pants and stepped outside. It was a beautiful night so I wandered out through the trees and damned if I didn't hear somebody on a horse coming down the trail like they only had a second to get where they were going."

"Did you get a good look at him?" the host asked, coffee cup poised in midair, waiting.

"No, and that's a funny thing. I thought I could see the trail, but my view must have been blocked by trees or branches, because the sound was right there and then it sounded on down the trail and was gone, but I didn't see anything."

My friend didn't mention to his visitor his own experiences with the phantom horse, not knowing how it might be accepted.

Phantom or ghost animals are not the everyday experiences of everyone. Humanlike apparitions seem a little more acceptable in our society. Our literature is resplendent with ghost stories, of apparitions seen by one or several people in a variety of settings. On occasion, the apparitions appear to be very substantial and at other times transparentlike replicas of a deceased relative or friend. Not infrequently, communication takes place between the phantom and the observer.

Acceptance of this phenomenon depends on one's belief

system and, particularly, on one's personal experiences. Persons who either gave the phenomenon little thought or simply rejected its validity have become strong believers as a result of their personal experiences. Those who have given at least some credence to these events usually try to find some theory that is comfortable to their rationality. This is not so difficult today in light of recent scientific findings which demonstrate that the world presented by our physical senses is not quite what it seems.

The new physics has revealed that the closer we examine physical substance, the more it eludes us. Investigation of matter under an electron microscope takes us from cells to molecules, to atoms, and into the world of subatomic particles. Particles disappear into energy fields. Aware that what we normally perceive is a peculiar arrangement of our minds, it becomes easier to accept the idea that the real nature of any object resides somewhere beyond its appearance to our senses. This recognition, coupled with the idea of a nonphysical mind no longer dependent on an organic brain, allows one to consider that life may go on with or without a physical body. That one may be able to perceive some other level or state of reality isn't too difficult to ponder within this conceptual framework.

I am reminded of the famous French chemist who refused to look into one of the early microscopes because he was quite sure there were no "bugs" in the human blood. And while it may be presumptive to suggest that most people are willing to give up the reality of physical substance, very few would argue today that what we experience through our physical senses is more than a fraction of what is perceivable.

Yet that expanding world of possibilities, where things are not what they seem, remains for the most part one available only to the human mind. When we tire of these cerebral exercises, we want our world of trees and lakes and dogs and mockingbirds to be in place. That the creature world may have experiences beyond those we have assigned them may be disconcerting to us. Ghost animals are one such phenomenon. When we personally experience animals performing roles other than those with which we are accustomed, the event is not easily forgotten.

Angus McDougall, the sculptor, years after the event talked about his phantom horse. He and his brother Ken were sons of the famous Dr. William McDougall, professor of psychology at Harvard for a number of years and director of the psychology department at Duke University at the time of his death in 1938.

When Angus was sixteen and Ken thirteen, the family held a picnic supper near an old deserted New England farmhouse located in the White Mountains. They were driven there by a Miss Baird, whose father owned the farm. The road, long unused, was so rough, however, that they finished the journey on foot.

The ancient two-room house stood in the middle of an overgrown pasture atop a hill, a gaunt, desolate sight against the sky. The adults settled on a spot with a view some distance from the house and made preparations for the meal. The boys went ahead to explore the old, abandoned structure.

The shingle roof was still intact, but the only door hung inward by a broken hinge. Only an earth floor remained inside, but there was a stair leading to the attic. Ken climbed to the attic while Angus walked around to the back of the house.

"There, several elderberry bushes had grown up over the roof forming a sort of tunnel or passage against the wall," Angus told a reporter years later. "I stepped inside this passage, and at once heard a horse snorting and kicking against the house." He thought at first that it was his brother playing a trick on him, but Ken appeared from around a corner of the house. Together they heard the horse snorting and pawing. The sound was desperate and loud.

They went back into the house, but it was as empty as before. "We stood staring at one another in utter bewilderment. Ken turned very white in the face, and no doubt I did, too. Without speaking, we walked slowly back to rejoin the picnic party by the cliff.''

Miss Baird was telling the sad history of the place when the boys arrived. Many years before, she said, the tenants to whom her father had rented the property decided to pull stakes and move west. They loaded all of their belongings in a single wagon. Left behind on the land was an old white horse that they believed would be too weak to make the journey.

Evidently, the horse went into the house to seek shelter from a storm, the door swung closed, and it was trapped inside. Mr. Baird found the carcass of the old horse when he came out in the spring to inspect his property. He buried it under the earthen floor of the house.

The entity that visited Norma and Tom Kresgal one night was entirely beneficient and well known. It was their long-dead pet collie Corky, and they credit him with saving their lives.

Writing for the *National Enquirer*, Miss Nicole Lieberman, a member of the American Society for Psychical Research and long-time lecturer on psychic phenomena, told the story of the Kresgals and their miraculous escape from death.

It seems that Norma found the dog under strange circumstances. She and Tom had recently been married and were living on a farm in New York State. A neighbor called and asked her to sit with his sick wife while he went to town for medicine. He returned in half an hour, and Norma started walking home. After a short distance, she experienced the sensation of not being alone. She stopped, looked around, saw nothing, and continued walking.

But the feeling persisted, and for a reason she could not explain, she felt compelled to leave the path and move into the forest. Fifty feet ahead she discovered a large collie lying stretched out with his neck red with blood.

He was still alive and wagged his tail feebly when she stroked his head. He was much too large for her to carry, so she rushed home for help. She and her husband's father took the dog to a veterinarian, who was able to remove a bullet from the dog's throat, but there was permanent damage to the throat box and he was never able to bark in a normal way.

No one claimed the dog, and Norma named him Corky. He was her close companion for years. When he died, they buried him under a tree on the farm.

Two years later, the Kresgals moved to New York City into an upstairs apartment in a two-family house.

They had lived in the apartment only a few months "when I was suddenly awakened one night by a strange sound," Mrs. Kresgal told Miss Lieberman. "It was Corky's hoarse bark. I thought I was dreaming and was about to go back to sleep when I heard him again—loud and clear."

Norma got out of bed and opened the bedroom door. She was met by great clouds of smoke. She roused Tom and they were able to get themselves and their landlord from the house before it was engulfed in flames.

"The tears were running down my face. Tom, thinking I was upset about our things being destroyed, told me not to worry because we were insured.

"He didn't know I cried in gratitude—thanking God with all my heart for letting my Corky come back to me long enough to rouse me—before it was too late."

It probably was not a matter of life and death when Lowanda Cady of Wichita, Kansas, was visited by her deceased dog, Jock, but he was welcome, nonetheless. She lived in an apartment complex, and several of the apartments in her section of the city were being entered, although it was primarily food from refrigerators that was being taken. Late one night she was roused from a deep sleep by the agitated barking of Jock. There were hurried footsteps in the rooms below her, a door was opened, and then sounds of someone running, accompanied by the barking dog. Mrs. Cady investigated and discovered that an intruder had been helping himself to the contents of her refrigerator. She started to look for Jock and stopped, having temporarily forgotten in the excitement that her pet had died three months before.

We are more likely to hear stories about experiences with domestic pets than wild animals. However, several years ago, while conducting a meditation retreat near Bear Creek Canyon in Colorado, I had the good fortune to see a phantom deer.

It should be explained that the site of the retreat was unusual in several ways. On the property are five of the largest blue spruces I have ever seen. They tower above all other trees in the area and are believed to be inhabited by a very high spirit who watches over the property. Because of the presence of this spirit, it is known as a healing place and was known as such by the American Indians before the white man came.

Several of us go there at least once each year for a week or so to relax, meditate, and "get it back together again." We have had some unforgettable experiences and it is always a delight to share with the wildlife that abounds there—deer, porcupines, ground squirrels, chipmunks, gray squirrels, birds of many kinds, and even skunks, who come close because they know they are loved and will be protected. Several years ago we constructed a shrine of white quartz from Bald Mountain to St. Francis, the patron saint of animals. We are sure the animals understand why we built the shrine.

One of the large spruces stands at the edge of the road through the property, and I have found this to be a particularly good place to meditate at night. Sitting with my back against the huge tree, I experience contentment, peace, and distinctive high vibrations. On this occasion I had slipped outside alone after a lively philosophical discussion in front of the fireplace. It was a hauntingly beautiful night, full of stars and magic, and I decided to meditate on my special piece of earth.

I had not meditated for long when something made me open my eyes. Not twenty-five feet from me, walking slowly along the road, was a deer. At first I thought it might be the large buck I had encountered in the woods that day. I had come upon him in a small clearing. We looked at each other for a few moments, then he went on grazing while I passed not more than twenty feet from him.

But as the deer drew closer I realized it was much smaller than the buck I had seen earlier. It seemed to be aware of my presence, for it paused on the path and seemed to be looking in my direction. When it stopped, I was startled to find that not only was I looking at the deer but I was also looking through it. The deer appeared real enough except for the transparent quality of the body, for I could clearly see the shadowy bushes on the edge of the road directly through him.

I mentally asked him to come closer, but his only response was a momentary pause to look back in my direction as he continued unhurriedly up the path in the moonlight. A hundred or so feet up the road he turned into the woods and disappeared. I have not seen him since, and yet on another night beside the tree I felt the soft, chamoislike nose of a deer, but that was all, a touch, and nothing was to be seen.

I don't recall mentioning the experience to anyone at the time, but during our retreat the following year, the subject came up quite unexpectedly. We were sitting in our usual evening half-circle around the fireplace when a guest asked if any of us had made contact with the phantom animals in the area. Our visitor was a young Irish-Brazilian Indian who had found his way deep into the Amazon Jungle in search of his maternal grandfather, the shaman of a small tribe known as "the people of the jaguar." There John Browne, who had trained as a jungle fighter in Vietnam, remained for three years in intensive training as replacement for his grandfather as secular-religious leader of the remote jungle community. Finally, realizing he would not be content to spend the remainder of his life as a shaman, Browne found his way back to western civilization. In the course of his initiatory training, however, he developed certain psychic powers, an acute awareness of nature, and an ability to perceive more than physical substance.

As he had experienced the phantom animals, Browne was pleased with my unusual deer story.

How did Browne explain the phantom animals?

"Animals in many ways are more closely aligned to the Group Soul than we are," Browne said. "But that closeness is one of the earth and their understanding is through the oneness they experience with all of nature.

"When they die," he continued, "their essence may be more strongly attached to physical existence than that of most humans. It may take them some time to experience reality beyond the earth plane. They linger here in their astral state until a sufficient part of their being is ready to move on. The earth plane is inhabited by many phantom animals but most people are not aware of them, although their own kind may be."

This appears to be the case in the story of a remarkable cat named Fingal. Several years ago, the English magazine *Prediction* related that Fingal had a highly developed sense of sympathy, responsibility, and affection for other pets. One pet was a turtle who had a habit of falling backward on his back and then was unable to struggle upright. When this occurred, Fingal would run excitedly to some member of the family and insist on their effecting an immediate rescue.

The cat would stay close by the cage if one of the rabbits got sick, keeping vigil until the crisis had passed. But when a human got sick, Fingal would keep his distance until he or she was better. This was considered an omen by the family.

Fingal kept a regular schedule. According to his owner, Celia Dale, "he liked to go out in the evening, stay an hour, and return punctually at nine o'clock. Then he would tap loudly on the French window to be let in."

Shortly after Fingal died, the tapping at the French window commenced again. It would be so insistent that the family would open the window. It would then cease.

On several occasions they were convinced they heard purrs from Fingal's favorite yellow cushion.

One afternoon a friend of the family brought her Siamese cat along for a visit. When the cat approached the chair containing Fingal's yellow cushion, he arched his back in fright. His eyes seemed to follow something as it moved toward the window. When the window was opened, the visiting feline—apparently aware that the original occupant of the chair had left—settled down on the vacated cushion.

One cat continued to be seen by a number of people many years after its death. The British writer Elliot O'Donnell relates the tale of the phantom cat in his book *Animal Ghosts*. The story was told to him by Mrs. Louise Marlowe.

Shortly after the turn of the century, Mrs. Marlowe was visiting a friend in the Yorkshire village of Congleton. One day, while taking a ride in a pony cart, they stopped near the ruins of an old abbey to pick wild roses. As the women approached the abbey gates, they saw perched on top of a hedge post a large, magnificent white cat.

"I wonder if it would let us pet it?" Mrs. Marlowe speculated.

They approached the cat, but it suddenly leaped into the air and disappeared. The women were bewildered, for the grass was cut too short to conceal the cat, but it was nowhere to be seen.

Two evenings later they drove down the same path and once again saw the white cat sitting regally on its post. The cat observed their approach with a friendly demeanor, but as they drew close, the animal slowly faded away. They stopped for tea in the village and mentioned the case of the disappearing cat to a waitress. The only response was a knowing smile, but a woman at the next table asked if it had been a large white cat.

"Good gracious sakes!" she then remarked. "You drove by the right time to see Congleton's ghost cat!"

The woman went on to say that she had lived in the

village more than fifty years and remembered the cat when it was alive. It had belonged to a Mrs. Winge, a housekeeper at the abbey. She was devoted to her pet. One day the animal disappeared and she was certain it had fallen victim to a dog pack. She was surprised, then, to hear meowing at the door a short time later. Joyfully she ran to the door to let the pet inside, but no matter how much she coaxed, he wouldn't enter.

The cat stood at her door for a time and then disappeared. At first she thought he was just flighty after his experience, but the same scene happened night after night. Each night Mrs. Winge opened the door, but the cat refused to come inside. Finally, one night by bright moonlight, the housekeeper saw her beloved pet simply dissolve away. Mrs. Winge was quite upset by the realization that her cat was now a ghost and she refused to answer its meowing at the door. Soon she left the neighborhood, telling friends that she liked live cats, but she didn't enjoy being visited by a dead one.

The woman at the tea shop concluded her tale by saying that this happened forty years before, but the sight of the ghost-cat remained a well-known phenomenon in the village.

In *The Book of Sunnybank*, Terhune tells of Rex, his ghost collie. Rex was a huge crossbreed and from puppyhood he was completely devoted to Terhune. Rex's favorite and only resting place was a spot in the hallway outside his master's study. He was not allowed in the dining room but he would watch the family at mealtime through the French windows from the veranda behind his master's chair.

Rex died in 1916, and during the summer of 1917, a friend of Terhune's came for the first time in several years for a visit. One afternoon, Terhune and the friend, the Reverend Appleton Grannis, were talking while seated at the dining-room table. Terhune's back was toward the French windows.

As they left the room, the minister commented, ''I thought I knew all of your dogs, but there's one I never saw until now. The big dog with the short fawn-colored coat and a scar across his nose. This dog has been standing outside the window staring in at you all the time we've been in this room. He's gone now. Which of your dogs is he?''

Rex, who had been dead a year, was the only dog who fitted his description. Grannis, however, had never seen Rex when he was alive, nor had Terhune mentioned him.

Another friend of Terhune's, Henry A. Healy, had made a study of Rex, for he was involved in studies on the problems of crossbreeding. One evening, he and his wife called on the Terhunes. As they were leaving, Healy remarked, ''You know, Bert, I wish there were some creature so utterly devoted to me as Rex is to you. I watched him as he lay at your feet. He kept looking up into your face every minute with a queer kind of devotion.''

''Good Lord, man! Rex has been dead for more than two years!'' Terhune exclaimed.

Healy was upset by his failure to remember. He frowned and finally said, ''Yes, I remember now,'' and he hesitated several seconds before adding, a little defiantly, ''Just the same, I would swear he was lying in the firelight at your feet all evening!''

Terhune noted that one of his Sunnybank collies, Bruce, lived for four years after Rex's death. During those years, Bruce was the only dog allowed in the study. Bruce never crossed the stretch of hallway that had been Rex's resting place. When Bruce entered the study he very carefully detoured around this spot as though to avoid something lying there. This was witnessed, Terhune stated, by a number of guests.

The late Dr. Nandor Fodor, the famous psychoanalyst who was acclaimed for his contributions to parapsychology, told in his book *Between Two Worlds* of the experience of Mrs. Henry Wipperman of Howard Beach, Long Island, New York. Mrs. Wipperman had two dogs, Skippy and Teddy. Skippy died from asthma and was buried in the yard of the home. That same evening, Skippy's familiar and distinctive wheeze was heard in the house. Not only did it claim the attention of Mrs. Wipperman and her mother, but Teddy raised his ears and searched the house for his playmate.

Seven years later, Teddy died. "I broke down crying and patted his head. He let out a big sigh," Mrs. Wipperman told Dr. Fodor. "The next day he was dead and we buried him. That evening I heard the special pant he developed when he became sick. I was embarrassed to mention it, but when I heard it again I asked Mother, 'Did you hear him?' She said yes, she had heard him, but did not want to tell me lest it upset me."

Dr. Fodor explained that hallucination was not the answer in this case. Not only was Skippy's wheeze heard independently by both women but also by Teddy.

Sometimes it seems that pets return momentarily to this plane of life in order to perform a certain task. In their book *The Strange World of Animals and Pets*, Vincent and Margaret Gaddis state that in 1940 Mrs. Ruth Whittlesey, the wife of a Protestant minister, was serving as superintendent of a convalescent hospital in Hawthorne, California.

In March of that year she was summoned to the hospital in the middle of the night to be with a patient who was dying. She was close enough to the hospital to walk, but she had to cross a lonely area with no houses or streetlights. As she moved from the lighted into the unlighted section, a car containing two men pulled up alongside of her. She started to run but the car followed her.

At that moment Mrs. Whittlesey's huge collie Nigel raced up and planted himself between her and the car. The men took one look at the dog and took off in a hurry. Nigel stayed with her until she reached a lighted area and then he was gone. As she recovered from her fright, it suddenly dawned on her that the big collie had died several months earlier. Mrs. Whittlesey wrote the Gaddises: "My husband is the minister of a well-known Protestant church. We are not superstitious or overly imaginative—

but we know that sometimes God moves in mysterious ways.''

''So above, so below; so below, so above'' is an ancient adage. In our lack of knowledge we may place too much emphasis on the distinctions between life during and after death whereas life may be life whenever it takes place and the differences may be ones of observation rather than of wise perception. Today we are witnessing a complete reassessment of the human potential and are allowing far greater possibilities of growth and accomplishment than we dared imagine even a few short years ago. Would we equate this expanded inner universe with a single life form, the human, and imagine that it alone moves toward some faroff but accessible goal?

Perhaps we should remember a prayer first uttered by St. Basil, Bishop of Caesarea, in A.D. 370:

''O God, enlarge within us the sense of fellowship with all living things, our little brothers to whom Thou has given this earth as their home in common with us. May we realize that they live not for us alone, but for themselves and for Thee, and that they love the sweetness of life even as we, and serve Thee better in their place than we in ours.''

CHAPTER EIGHT

Do Animals Commit Suicide?

We may assume that animals do not understand the nature of death. While they may miss a mate after it's gone or grieve in the absence of a departed owner, we may dismiss this behavior as not reflective of any insight into the meaning of death. But how can we explain an animal's awareness of death occurring to its master many miles away if it had no comprehension of its meaning? Equally puzzling are those cases where animals obviously seek their own death, or will risk their lives to save that of a person, or will visit a grave to pay their last respects, and even dying themselves shortly thereafter.

The September 1956 issue of *Fate* told a story of a bird lover named William Milburn who lived in Durham, England. During his life he had kept many wild birds, but during his waning years only one bird remained, a song thrush. She refused to fly away and burst into song whenever the old man appeared on the scene and sometimes would perch on his shoulders or head.

Milburn became ill with influenza and the thrush sang very little. On the day the man died, and for the three days that his coffin was in the house, the bird did not sing at all. Yet as the pallbearers raised the casket to take it from the house, the thrush began to sing, and she sang her heart out in a requiem as the procession moved away. When the hearse left for the cemetery, she was silent again, for she, too, was dead.

The June 1946 edition of *Reader's Digest* tells the story of a small mongrel puppy that was adopted by the Seabees in the Gilbert Islands. She was fed canned milk through an eyedropper until large enough to eat on her own. Her foster parents, the crew of an LCT, named her Puddles and spoiled her as only lonely people do.

But the time came when the LCT had served its time. Orders came for it to be junked and sent to the bottom. Another crew attempted to adopt Puddles, but she refused, and regulations prohibited her from being taken to the States. Aboard another craft, Puddles only whined and refused to eat, so the crew allowed her to go back and watch as the condemned craft was salvaged of equipment. From the beach she watched sadly as the men stripped the craft and finally towed it out to sea to be sunk. When the men returned to the beach after sinking the vessel, Puddles was still there, but she was watching no longer, for she was dead.

The Gambill Wild Goose Reservation near Paris, Texas, was named for its founder, John Gambill. Gambill once nursed a wounded gander back to health and the following autumn the gander returned with twelve geese that became quite tame, according to Joe F. Combs, feature writer for the Beaumont, Texas, *Enterprise*.

The next year the number of geese was in excess of a hundred, and by the time Gambill died in 1962, it was estimated that more than three thousand geese wintered in safety on the reservation. As Gambill died in a Paris hospital, hundreds of geese from the reservation flew into Paris and circled around and around the hospital, honking their requiem. Somehow, someway they knew.

What does death represent to an animal? At this point in time, perhaps we have no way of knowing. Perhaps, as with people, it is an individual thing to be met by different animals in their own fashion. Some animals seem to be unaware of its approach, while some make preparations for the event; for example, certain dogs and cats search for places to be alone at the time of death, knowing that it is imminent.

Writing at the turn of the century about animals, E. D. Buckner, M.D., stated: "Almost everything in the whole universe is common to both man and the lower animals. They are subject to the general laws of gravitation and force, and are in danger from falls and all impressions of violence. They are subject to disease, injuries, pains, and liable to mental diseases, such as melancholy and insanity. They need nourishment, a proper habitation, protection from wanton abuse, cruelty, or any form of suffering which may possibly be avoided. They have a nervous system which is equally sensitive to all the impressions made upon the body. They are conscious of a liberty to act or not to act, and have a desire for comforts and happiness. They have a social feeling and a desire to love and be loved, and their good and bad dispositions are formed according to their environments, danger, and the dread of exposure. The strange feeling of affection enables them to overcome the fear of risks, even of death itself, in order to save the lives of friends. And they show their consciousness of having performed such moral acts by their manifestation of joy for any approbation bestowed on them. They not only give themselves as a sacrifice, but make intercession for the welfare and protection of others."

Certainly intercession was the case when forty seconds before a raging wall of mud and water crashed into their home, Clem Gfoerer and his family were saved by a loyal German shepherd they had rescued from death only two years earlier.

The quick-thinking pet—ironically named Last Chance—was adopted by the Gfoerers shortly before it was to be put to sleep. It smashed down part of the Gfoerer's bedroom door, got inside, and started tugging frantically on Mrs. Gfoerer's arm. "When I jumped from the bed, I froze in fright. Suddenly I was knee-deep in muck and mud. 'Oh, my God, we're all drowning . . . we're being flooded!' I started screaming," the Cathedral City, California, woman explained.

Outside the home, a tremendous storm was raging and

tons of water barreled down the San Jacinto Mountains, heading for their home at an approximate speed of sixty miles an hour.

After waking Mrs. Gfoerer, the three-year-old dog headed for the bedroom of the seventeen-year-old son, Bill. "I wasn't even thinking and Last Chance was trying to tell me to get my son out," said Mrs. Gfoerer. "I started screaming, 'Billy! Billy! Get up!' "

While Billy was getting up, his father got the shock of his life. "I looked through a picture window and saw a giant wall of water coming right at us," Gfoerer said.

Frantic, the family and the dog moved to the rear of the house, slamming doors behind them. "We just got to the back of the house when the water came right through and over the top of the house," Gfoerer explained. "Within forty seconds after the dog woke Pat, the house filled with water. It would have killed Billy instantly. He would have been buried alive in mud. After the water broke the windows, mud filled his room. We found splinters of his bed in the mud in other rooms of the house. Billy and my wife had to stand on a bed to keep their heads above water." As six more waves of water tore through the house, Pat and Billy clung to the ceiling rafters above the bed.

"Finally, I broke two windows to make a path for the water," Gfoerer said. "Then another wave came through the house and it pushed us out the window and carried us with it for about twenty-five or thirty yards until we landed on high ground."

Two years before this occurrence, the Gfoerer family had rescued Last Chance from a mean owner who had brutalized the dog and was planning on putting him to sleep.

"When I heard that his owner was going to put him to sleep, I said, 'My God! I'll take him.' We gave him his chance to live so we named him Last Chance. In a sense he was our last chance, for if it hadn't been for him, we would have all been dead," Gfoerer stated.

If fear and the instinct of survival were all that had

motivated Last Chance, he would simply have fled the house. Instead, he stayed and risked his life in order to save the lives of his owners. Saving lives while risking one's own does not in any sense indicate a death wish. However, it does imply a knowledge of the nature of death and the willingness to give up life in order to save others.

One must wonder if the mass march of lemmings to the sea where they swim off shore until they drown is collective suicide in order to save those that remain behind from starvation.

Apparently, there are years when lemmings' reproductive cycles run amuck and millions upon millions of the little creatures—which are sexually mature at twelve days old and have only a twenty-day gestation period—soon run out of food supplies. When this happens, an exodus to the sea takes care of the food problem for a time. Is this seeming sacrifice a conscious one on the part of the lemmings? Animal behaviorist Vitus B. Droscher thinks not.

In his book *The Friendly Beast*, Droscher points out that Africa used to present a somewhat comparable phenomenon. Before the white man with his rifles thinned out the great herds, lemminglike mass increases used to take place from time to time among springboks. Migrations of up to fifty thousand of these gazelles would head for the Namid Desert in Southwest Africa, where they died miserably. Sailors have also sighted swarms of locusts over the middle of the Atlantic, two thousand miles from their birthplace in Africa. But the insects' stamina would give out and they would drop by the billions into the sea.

"But are such phenomena really suicide as we human beings understand the term?" Droscher asks, and answers, "Not at all. For the locusts were bent on finding new land—like Columbus. But in these mass flights they were at the mercy of the wind and, when driven westward, had nowhere to alight. The springboks had exhausted their usual grazing grounds and were desperately searching for new pastures. The case of the lemmings is rather similar.''

Lemmings are good swimmers. They will cross rivers and lakes to find food. ''But when they come to a body of water, they do not, as they are reported to, plunge into it blindly,'' Droscher explains. ''Rather, they change their otherwise straight course and run up and down the shoreline looking for a flat beach. Then they move into the water with extreme caution. But if they find themselves on a precipitous coast with no favorable spots for entering the water, hunger and migratory madness will leave them no choice. Then, but only then, do they take the leap as if commiting an act of extreme desperation.''

But—as with people—self-destruction emerges in a vastly different way in the story of Mac, an English shepherd mixture owned by Bill Myers of Dallas. Mac and Bill were inseparable for six years before Bill left home to join the Army. Mac would grieve for Bill during his long absences and become uncontrollably excited when Bill returned home on leave.

Then, one day, word was received by the family that Bill had been killed in Vietnam. Three days before the family was informed, Mac refused to eat and sat unmoving in the yard and staring off into space. The family bought the dog all of his favorite foods, but to no avail. They placed him in the car and drove him to a wooded park where they invited him to go on a hike with them, but Mac slumped listlessly beside the car. Slowly the heartbroken animal wasted away and, two weeks after Bill was killed, Mac died.

The story of Mac presents several interesting questions. How did the dog know, even before the family knew, that Bill was dead? In seeking death, what did it represent to him? Was the act of self-destruction a way of turning off the pain, or did he somehow believe that through death he would find Bill again? As with humans, can the fear of death be less than the fear of continued living?

On the other hand, researchers have found that chimpanzees demonstrate a haunting fear of death. Citing the experiments of Dr. Adrian Kortlandt in the Congo jungle, Vitus B. Droscher states in *The Friendly Beast*: "We will recall the chimpanzee's fear of death expressed in his drawing back from dead animals, from the arm or leg of a member of his own species, even from sleeping animals and lifeless images. Such fear is of an utterly different nature from the fears manifested by other animals. . . . But whether chimpanzees with this degree of consciousness of death are ever compelled to suicide, no one can say at present. . . . It may also be that chimpanzees have a much stronger fear of death than men and for this reason alone are incapable of suicide. To the superficial view, the anthropoid ape's fright reaction at the sight of a corpse is certainly far more violent than ours. In this sense these animals evidently see the situation far more realistically than a man entangled in delusions and emotional confusions who wants to take his own life."

In her article "Magic Zoology in the British Isles," published in *Tomorrow* magazine, summer 1953, Mrs. Grace N. Isaacs tells a story of a man named Henry who owned a large cattle ranch near Trelawney. He cared a great deal for his animals and would not turn their care over to others. He died unexpectedly and his coffin was placed in a wagon for the journey to the church and cemetery. The distance from the house to the gate of the estate was great, and along this route a large number of mourners were gathered. During the procession the mourners were suddenly startled by the moaning and bellowing of cattle. Herds of animals gathered from the surrounding pastures and stood in long lines along the fence bordering the drive. They tossed their heads, pawed the ground, and lamented in tones quite unlike their usual lowing.

A cat paid his respects at the grave of his master according to a story in the autumn 1963 issue of *Tomorrow*, an English magazine. The correspondent stated that his grandfather and a cat named Bill were extremely close. The cat followed him by day and slept in his bed at night.

The man was seriously hurt in a railway accident and for a week lay in a hospital several miles from his home. He died in the hospital and his body was taken from there to the church and then to the churchyard for burial. As the rites were finished, an uncle of the writer looked up and saw Bill approaching the grave. He moved with dignity to the grave, stood for a short time looking at the coffin, and having passed his respects, turned and headed home.

In his book, *The Soul of the Ape*, Eugene Marais tells of a young chacma baboon whose infant had to be taken away from her for medical treatment. The mother screamed almost unceasingly for three days while Marais futilely battled to save the baby's life. When the dead young baboon was returned to the still-distraught mother, she "approached the body, making the chacma sounds of endearment, and touched it twice with her hands. She then put her face close to the back of the dead infant, touching its skin with her mouth, at the same time moving her lips in the usual manner. Immediately afterwards, she got up, uttered a succession of cries, walked to a corner, and sat down quietly in the sun, apparently taking no more interest in the body."

Gilbert Manley, while observing the chimpanzee colony at the London Zoo, saw one female clasp an injured infant to her breast and carry it about with her everywhere for some time, refusing to allow the keepers to take it from her. Eventually, while Manley was watching, the baby died and the mother simply put it down and never touched it again.

Lyall Watson relates in *The Romeo Error* that contrary to the above incidents, "there are many accounts of mothers carrying around dead young individuals until they decompose." He adds, "There are stories of elephants and buffalo remaining with a stricken herd member and attempting fruitlessly to lift the dead animal back onto its feet." There are ways—some of them may even be instinctive—in which social animals can assist a young or injured group member.

Konrad Lorenz in *On Aggression* relates how grayling geese will stand with outspread wings over a dying friend, hissing defensively. He adds, "I observed the same behavior on the occasion of an Egyptian goose killing a graylag gosling by hitting it in the head with its wing; the gosling staggered toward its parents and collapsed, dying of cerebral hemorrhage. Though the parents could not have seen the deadly blow, they reacted in the way described."

Regarding this incident, Watson commented that "the defensive behavior under these circumstances was appropriate; it had survival value for the gosling, who may only have been temporarily concussed. There comes a point, however, where the species members can do no more for their fellow. Recognition of this moment may have to be learned."

George Schaller, in his account of the mountain gorillas of Kisori, *The Year of the Gorilla*, tells of a young animal that refused to leave the body of its adult companion. "It was a brutal choice for such an infant to have to make: escape man and enter the forest to wander alone in search of its group, a task for which it was unprepared, or cling to the last vestige of its former happy group life, a dead leader who for the first time failed to protect it. Finally, the youngster was captured, only to die later in London Zoo."

An awareness of death and the consequences of suicide seem to be clearly demonstrated in the story of Rags. Few dogs have been called upon to help a large number of people as was Rags. She was the only inhabitant of Sing Sing Prison who was there by choice.

Rags turned herself in at the gray somber walls during a cold autumn day and was to serve twelve years, becoming a legend in her own time. A small mongrel, part Scottie and part wire-haired terrier, Rags spent her days cheering up the dismal atmosphere of the prison. She worked out a set of tricks, stunts, mimicry, and acrobatics to entertain the men. A large part of each day was spent making the rounds of the shops, the cell blocks, and the hospital.

Rags befriended them all but was careful never to show partiality to anyone. She completely ignored the guards, the warden, and visitors. She would eat at a different table in the mess hall each day, systematically rotating in order not to miss a table. She left the prison compound at the end of the day to sleep in the warden's home but would return in the evening if there was going to be entertainment or a performance, never failing to know when this would be. Warden Laives ordered the guards to let her in and out of the locked gates whenever she wished.

Rags was particularly sensitive to a despondent, brooding prisoner. She would rub her head against him, perform all kinds of acts to cheer him up, and then lead him to a group so he would not be alone.

One night Rags did not leave the cellblocks. She followed one of the prisoners to his cell and remained in front of it until morning. The prisoner had been refused a pardon and, discouraged, he had decided that no one cared what happened to him. He was determined to end it all that night by hanging himself with his bed sheet.

Rags never gave the man that chance. Every time he tried to slip out of his bunk, the dog would growl, and he knew if he went farther, Rags would bark and bring the guard on the run. He finally decided that at least Rags cared what happened to him and he would give himself another chance at life.

Spot apparently was aware that death was pending the night he saved a widow and her two children from fire. Spot was dedicated to his life as a fire dog. He rode the fire trucks and watched the battles against raging fires as the mascot of Headquarters Company Station in Camden, New Jersey.

On this particular evening, Spot changed his sleeping quarters from the fire station to the home of Mrs. Anna Souders, the widowed mother of his two playmates, eleven-year-old Nora and eight-year-old Maxwell. The Souder home was across the street from the fire station.

Shortly after Spot made his switch, he was awakened by smoke. He rushed around the house barking a frantic warning. He then threw his weight against the door of Mrs. Souder's bedroom. The dog ran to the bed and pulled the blankets from the sleeping woman. She roused her children, flung open a window, and called for help. She then collapsed, unconscious, but Spot remained at the window, barking. His barking attracted the attention of a patrolman, and all members of the family were rescued in time. Spot refused to leave the house until the children and Mrs. Souder were safe.

Jack, the dalmation mascot of Engine Company 105 of Brooklyn, New York, received the Medal of Valor from the Humane Society of New York for saving a young child's life. One day the fire truck on which Jack was riding wheeled out of the station in pursuit of a fire. Suddenly a three-year-old child dashed in front of the truck. The driver slammed on his brakes, but the weight and momentum of the truck was too great. Jack leaped to the pavement, shot in front of the truck, and rolled the boy out of the way just in the nick of time.

Deborah Palmer of Wichita, Kansas, brought the aging female Doberman home from the city pound because she felt pity for the scrawny dog. Little did she realize that her gesture of compassion would save the lives of her daughter and three other girls.

Just a week after bringing home the shy dog—who the family named Sheba—she was a hero. According to Dave Goodwin, a reporter for the *Wichita Eagle*, six girls were playing in the street when a car under repair started in gear and lurched toward the girls. One child was killed when trapped under the car and another girl was slightly injured. But, thanks to Sheba, four of the girls escaped unharmed.

Goodwin explained that the dog was on a leash at the time of the incident. She saw the car lurch toward the girls and she pulled on the leash. Anissa Vaught was hanging on to the leash. One of the other girls was holding Anissa's hand and the hand of a third girl. A fourth girl had her arms around the third child. Sheba dragged all four girls to safety.

"Since Palmer brought Sheba home from the pound, the dog has had a special affection for Anissa [Palmer's daughter]," Goodwin stated. "When the child was restless at night, Sheba would lie at her side until she fell asleep, then return to her spot in the living room. Three nights ago, Anissa had an earache, but her cries didn't rouse her mother. Palmer was awakened by a nudge from a cold canine nose.

"I wouldn't take a million dollars for that dog," Goodwin quoted Palmer as saying.

Another unwanted animal, this one a kitten, is credited with saving the lives of three persons in a disastrous house fire.

According to Paul F. Levy, writing in a recent issue of the *National Enquirer*, Diane Malcolm found the hungry stray kitten and persuaded her sister-in-law, Jane Malcolm of Saint Clair, Michigan, to take it in until a home could be found for the animal. A few days later Diane was babysitting four-year-old Jennifer and one-year-old Holly while their parents were out of town.

"Both girls were asleep in their room and I had fallen asleep on the living-room couch," Diane told Levy. "At one A.M. a fire broke out in the basement and the house began filling with smoke, but I slept right through it and so did the girls."

The cat, however, realized something was wrong. He jumped on Diane's chest and started crying loudly. Diane woke up, ran to the children's room, and got them, along with the cat, out of the house.

She called the fire department from a neighbor's phone and the house was saved from total destruction. But Fire Chief Perry Westrick stated that "if they hadn't gotten out when they did, they might never have gotten out."

Needless to say, the kitten, which they named Boots, became a permanent member of the family instead of an unwanted guest. "He's part of the family now," Jane told Levy. "I think Boots knew what he was doing when he woke Diane up. He knew he was saving my children's lives.''

A London dog endeavored to save the life of its owner by pinpointing a malignant tumor and then trying to bite it off.

The respected British medical weekly, *The Lancet*, reported in March 1989, that a two-year-old cross between a Doberman pinscher and a collie, named Baby, ''may have saved her owner's life by prompting her to seek treatment when the lesion was still at a thin and curable stage,'' wrote Hywel Williams and Andres Pembroke, doctors at King's College Hospital in London.

They said the dog ignored other moles and marks on the woman but spent several minutes a day sniffing the tumor over a period of several months until the owner finally sought medical advice.

''It is unlikely that the dog was merely fascinated by the appearance of the melanoma since she could smell the lesion through the patient's clothing,'' the doctors wrote.

Baby's owner, Bonita Whitfield, forty-four, told Sky Television she was in her garden during the summer of 1988 wearing shorts when the dog twice tried to bite off the tumor.

''It's possible that a dog can pick out this particular tumor just as it smells explosives,'' Williams told Sky Television.

He said he would like to test the dog in blind trials on patients, adding: ''It seems rather amusing, but it's still theoretically possible.''

''There are many cases recorded of remarkable animal loyalty, and not a few have sacrificed their lives for their masters,'' Manly Palmer Hall explains in *The Inner Lives of Minerals, Plants, and Animals*. ''Many of the higher mammals are completely monogamous and, having created a family, protect it for life. Once they have mated, mandarin ducks are inseparable, and if one dies the other will probably commit suicide.''

Yet, as with people, not all animals are equal in their

sensitivity and awareness. Animals within the same species may demonstrate completely different behavior patterns. Some dogs—such as Mac—may become so distraught they no longer wish to live when their master dies. Yet the neighbor's dog doesn't seem to be aware, or care, when his master dies in the next room. On the other hand, perhaps we fail to pick up on the messages, for as Hall explains: "Because animals cannot vocalize their feelings as we do, it requires a degree of intuition and a great deal of skillful observation to estimate their inner lives."

CHAPTER NINE

Return From the Grave

Frank Talbert was profoundly but very contently tired. He stood looking out of his large picture window at a thunderstorm moving over the mountains to the north. He mused that it would be a good night to sleep. A fire to chase the early October chill, a needed rain falling outside, peaceful solitude, what more could he ask for? he wondered.

Talbert had spent the day thinning some of the timber from his property near Breckenridge, Colorado. A successful real-estate broker in Denver, Talbert had bought ten acres of mountain land and constructed a three-room cabin. He referred to it as his hideaway. Although he spent some weekends there with his family, he was particularly happy when he could get away by himself for a few days. On this occasion, he planned to spend a week and a half alone to work on the property.

He banked the fireplace for the night and went to bed. The wind had started up, rain pelted down on the cedar roof, and occasional lightning allowed him a brief glimpse of the rockface east of the cabin. But Talbert quickly drifted into sleep. How long he slept he wasn't sure, but a sound awakened him. It was still raining, the lightning had drawn closer, and the thunder now came in rolling crashes and crescendoes, but this was not the sound which jarred him awake. Somewhere outside a dog was barking. Talbert sat up in bed, listening. The bark came again, this time at some distance. He was starting to slide back down in the bed when the barking seemed but a few feet from the door. It was both a howl and a bark and Talbert decided the dog was in some kind of trouble and was asking for help, or perhaps simply wanted shelter from the storm.

He opened the door but could see only a few feet through the driving rain. He called, but there was no answer. Talbert was about to shut the door again when a flash of lightning provided him a glimpse of a dog not more than thirty feet away. He called to the animal, but instead of coming closer, the dog moved slowly away but giving a mournful, appealing howl while doing so. Obviously, Talbert decided, the dog wanted him to follow and he wondered if she had puppies that were exposed to the storm. He quickly slipped on his boots and into a hooded parka. The dog was waiting for him. Talbert was able to get within a few feet of the dog before it turned away, evidently expecting him to follow. He had been close enough to see by his flashlight beam that the dog appeared to be a red setter, only it had a white neck and chest.

But Talbert followed the dog only a few yards when everything around him turned red and a tremendous explosion nearly deafened him. Lightning had struck his cabin and a fire had started in the bedroom. He managed to haul some of his possessions outside, but in the rain and darkness, relieved only by the light from the fire and the headlights of his pickup truck, it was difficult work. Most of the cabin was destroyed and there was little he could do except watch the flames from his truck.

Only when he was preparing to leave and drive to the nearest neighbor's place did Talbert remember the dog. By this time the rain had stopped, the sky had partially cleared, and the moon provided some illumination. He looked for the setter, but the dog was not around. As he searched for the animal it dawned on Talbert that the lightning had struck the bedroom area and the reason the fire burned so intensely was because the mattress and bedding must have instantly ignited. If the dog had not coaxed him outside, he most likely would have died in that bed.

When he told his story to his neighbor, the man was perplexed. "The dog you describe sounds like Sandy," the man said, slowly shaking his head. "She was a setter but with that very unusual marking of a white chest and neck. . . ."

"That must be her, all right. My God, where is she? I think I have to thank her for my life!" Talbert exclaimed.

The neighbor didn't say anything for several moments. He stared at Talbert and then slumped in his chair. His voice was hardly audible as he whispered, "That won't be possible, Frank. She died more than two months ago."

Was Sandy still physically alive when she lured Frank Talbert away from danger? No, no mistake about her death; she had been buried near her owner's home. Could it have been another setter? Possible, of course, but one with the same markings as Sandy and living in the same area makes this possibility rather remote. Perhaps a dog from the same litter as Sandy? She was born in Texas and brought to Colorado when she was eight years old. Perhaps it was one of Sandy's pups and had the same markings? Sandy never had a litter; an operation prevented this. So, Talbert—and we—will never know. Yet Talbert will remember his visitor—whoever or whatever it may have been—for a long time. His neighbor gave him a picture of Sandy. He framed it and it sits on his desk in his home.

The Colorado mountains were the setting for a similar event a few years ago. The man to experience this strange happening is convinced his life was saved by a dog whose life he had saved when the animal was one year old. Only the dog had to come back from the grave to pay the debt. Robin Deland does not know how, but he has little doubt that his collie Jeff accomplished this feat.

On this particular night Deland was driving on an unpaved, narrow and winding road near Gunnison. He had started up a sharp incline when suddenly a dog appeared in his headlights, only a short distance ahead in the road. The animal stood there unmoving and Deland had to brake to a stop. He sat frozen in his seat, for the dog, now only a few feet away and clearly detailed by his car lights, was Jeff. Why was he so sure? Maybe only those who have had a pet as a constant companion for a dozen years can understand. Deland had found the young collie dying alongside a highway after having been struck by a vehicle. He rushed the dog to an animal hospital, and after extensive surgery, he nurtured the collie back to health. They were extremely close. Deland knew every hair on the dog's body. And Jeff was extremely large for his breed. He had a massive head but a somewhat short nose for a collie. Deland is quite certain that his rendezvous on a rocky mountain precipice was with Jeff, even though the dog had died six months prior to this incident.

He was so awed and bewildered by the presence of Jeff that Deland doesn't remember getting out of the car. He recalls walking toward the dog and he believes that he held out his hand and called Jeff's name. Almost within reach, the animal suddenly whirled away and walked slowly up the road toward the peak of the incline. Deland followed, trying to catch up with Jeff, trying to get close enough to touch him. He topped the incline, but just beyond, silhouetted by the moonlight, was a massive rock slide, burying the road. If his car had reached that point, it would have been certain death. There would have been no way he could have kept from plunging off the cliff in a drop of several hundred feet.

Deland said he doesn't know how long he stood on the edge of the precipice, staring at the rock slide and then to the dark depths below. He imagines that he might have been in a kind of trance, unable for several minutes to cope with the impact of the event. Shaking himself out of the spell, he remembers, he immediately looked around for Jeff and called out to him. But the dog had disappeared as mysteriously as he had suddenly come back into Deland's life.

Apparition? Hallucination? If seeing things that have no basis in reality, isn't it rather strange that the nonexistent Sandy and Jeff so appropriately saved two lives. If Talbert and Deland's hallucinations were so timely, can such experiences only occur without the benefit of witnesses?

There were several witnesses to the occurrences that pulled the Raymond Peters family from a certain death trap one recent December night.

Raymond and his wife Suzanne had turned in early, for both were exhausted. They had been kept up all night by one of their children who had an upset stomach. And the two previous nights they had worked into the wee hours on their income taxes. Bed was a welcome haven and they recall they were almost asleep by the time they stretched out in bed. But their sleep that night was fated to be even shorter.

Approximately four hours after retiring, both Raymond and Suzanne were awakened by a dog barking. Raymond recalls that still half-asleep he called out to his Scottie, Mac, to hush, and he remembers his wife saying, "What in the world is the matter with him?" But Mac was not to be ignored. Raymond explained that there wasn't any way they could fall back asleep, for the next instant, Mac was frantically barking almost in his ear. Raymond sat up, saying, "Damn it, Mac . . ." thinking the dog wanted to go outside to urinate. But then he smelled smoke. Instantly wide awake, he leaped out of bed. Their bedroom door was closed, and when they opened it, choking smoke had already filled the hallway. They could feel the heat of the fire in the ceiling and the far end of the hall was aflame, but it had not yet reached the children's bedroom.

They grabbed the still-sleeping youngsters in their arms and fled from the house. Their exit was none too soon, for minutes later, the old dwelling was engulfed in flames. The fire department had already been called by a neighbor who had been awakened, not by first seeing and smelling the fire, but by the barking dog. It had been so close, he said, that he first thought the dog was inside his own home. He then looked out the window for the dog and saw the flames. By the time the firemen arrived, the house was too far gone to save and they concentrated on keeping the fire from spreading. Raymond and Suzanna Peters lost all of their possessions but their family was safe.

Only when their neighbor said to them, "My God, you would never have made it if it hadn't been for your dog. I didn't know that you had gotten another dog after Mac died. . . . Where is he, Ray? Did he get out of the house?"

The Peterses looked at each other, speechless for several moments. Raymond is not sure what he said at this point, but he recalls that it felt as though his heart had stopped, and he was dizzy. He heard Suzanna say, "Raymond . . . oh, Raymond," as though frightened, and then himself saying, "It was Mac . . . I know Mac's bark. . . . We've never had any other dog." No need to look for the Scottie, for he had made his exit three months previously.

I can appreciate the bewilderment, the awe, and the lasting wonderment in having a beloved pet, seemingly lost forever by death, return. The experience, equally frightening and joyful, leaves in its wake a myriad of perplexing, emotional responses. Life is never quite the same again. New dimensions are added. The implications are not always understood, but old belief systems are forced into revision.

My experience of this nature happened with a dachshund we had raised from a pup and had for thirteen years. I have loved and shared with many kinds of animals all my life. They have enriched my life, and it would have been somewhat emptier except for them. Yet, it is doubtful that I would be writing this book if my experience with the dachshund, Phagen, had not occurred. It made great demands on me and I am grateful for this.

The story of Phagen's return after his death is told in

a later chapter, but I mentioned it here to explain my personal conviction that once a person has experienced the very real happening of the continued existence of a pet after its death, the fear of death—the seeming loss and separation—is never quite the same again.

Dr. Robert A. Bradley, a practicing physician in Denver and a pioneer in psychosomatic medicine and medical hypnosis, is a strong supporter of animal survival after death. In his book *Psychic Phenomena*, co-authored by his wife Dorothy, he relates a personal experience with animal immortality:

"There is a controversial discussion regarding the survival of animals after death. Our family does not question the premise since further evidence of survival after death came from a rather unexpected source. One of our dogs was a tiny two-pound Chihuahua who, when let outdoors in the winter, would shortly bark his piercing, shrill bark to be let back in. He hated the outdoors summer or winter and would make himself irritatingly obnoxious until let back in.

"It was just before Christmas. The winter weather had set in. The family was busy making holiday preparations and on this night was involved primarily in trimming the tree. We hadn't noticed that the little dog had been let out (he had not barked to be let in) until one of the children noticed that he was missing.

"A search for the dog was started immediately by the children, but to no avail. We all then joined in the search both indoors and out, because I had the definite feeling something was wrong with the dog. We systematically searched and called outside the house and, not finding him, began a systematic search inside.

"Dorothy and Seig remained at the Christmas tree, continuing to decorate. As the search party came to the hall where the tree was, Dorothy and Seig were surprised to hear us all worriedly wondering where the dog could be. They assured us they had heard his series of shrill barks just before we came and supposed we had found him. We asked them which direction the barking sounds came from? They both seemed confused and pointed vaguely up toward the center hall, somewhere. . . I immediately said, 'He's dead. That was an astral bark you heard! He's met something unfamiliar and is giving his usual hostile reaction.' I had the sudden conviction we would find him dead. I got a flashlight and carefully explored the dark corners outside the house, and sure enough, there he was, frozen to death, just outside the window within a few feet from where Seig and Dorothy were working trimming the tree. Fifteen to twenty minutes before on our first search I had stood practically at that spot and tapped on that window to ask Seig to turn on the outside lights. I must have been within inches of the dog at that time, but he was in a shadow where I couldn't see him. However, he was of a vivacious nature and had he been alive would have made himself known.

"Examination showed his tongue and throat to be frozen solid, his jaws frozen shut. How was it possible for Dorothy and Seig to have heard his series of vivacious, shrill barks just a few minutes before? And why were the sounds they heard coming from the opposite direction and from 'on high'?"

In *The Strange World of Animals and Pets*, Vincent and Margaret Gaddis tell the story of Freda Aston of Tulsa, Oklahoma, and a family dog, Fife, an English mastiff. When Freda was a young girl, the dog was badly mauled in a fight. His wounds were treated and he appeared to be recovering, but one morning he could not be found. The family was greatly concerned that the dog, then fifteen years old, might be lying helpless somewhere.

Then Miss Aston's mother had a dream in which she had a vision of Fife standing strong and proud in his prime. She saw him standing on a hill, happily wagging his tail. Then the dog looked down at his feet, and her eyes followed his and beneath him on the ground lay the battle-scarred body of Fife stretched out in death.

The following morning, her mother took Freda by the hand. "Come," she was quoted as saying, "we are going to find Fife.'' She told the child about her dream and they walked to a place closely resembling the scene, a group of hillocks, that she had seen in her vision. ''There lay the old body that had housed Fife's brave, loyal heart for so many years, just as she had seen it in her dream,'' Miss Aston wrote the authors.

Another unusual experience of an owner dreaming about the death of a pet was told by the famous British novelist Sir Rider Haggard, who wrote *King Solomon's Mines*. Sir Haggard's report on this experience and his signed affidavit appeared in the ''Proceedings'' of the British Society for Psychical Research on October 4, 1904.

Shortly after midnight on July 10, 1904, Haggard cried out in his sleep, and he started struggling and gasping for breath. His wife awakened him and he told her that the dream had started with a sense of depression, and then he seemed to be struggling for his life. As the dream became more vivid, he sensed that he was trapped inside the body of his black retriever named Bob. ''I saw Bob lying on his side among brushwood by the water,'' he reported. ''My own personality seemed to be arising in some mysterious manner from the body of the dog, who lifted up his head at an unnatural angle against my face. Bob was trying to speak to me, and not being able to make himself understood by sounds, transmitted to my mind in an undefined fashion the knowledge that he was dying.'' Haggard told his wife that he had a vision of a marshy area near their place.

Four days later, Sir Haggard found the dog's body about a mile from the house. It was floating in the Waverly River. It was discovered that the dog had been badly injured. A veterinarian stated that the skull had been fractured and the two front legs broken, and that it was likely the body had been in the water more than three days, probably since the night of July 9.

Haggard learned from two station hands that the dog likely had been struck by a train. They showed Haggard a spot near a trestle bridge where there was dried blood and part of a dog's collar that they found on Monday, July 11. Later that day they said they saw the dog's body floating below the bridge. It was determined that the dog was likely struck on the trestle bridge by a freight train from Harlesdon at about the time of Haggard's dream.

The survival of animals after death has been substantiated by those who have been in unusual states to offer verification. The reporting of out-of-the-body experiences has enjoyed recent widespread coverage by the news media. Oftentimes these reports are by persons who have sustained clinical deaths, have left their bodies, allegedly experienced other planes of existence, and then have returned to their bodies and related what happened during this time. Out-of-the-body occurrences, however, are not limited to sudden stoppages of vital functions. While lecturing to college classes on altered states of consciousness I sometimes ask for a show of hands from those who have in some fashion experienced awareness of themselves separate from their physical bodies. I have been amazed to learn that approximately one-third responded in the affirmative. And there have been those who have developed this skill or talent to the degree that they can voluntarily extract their consciousness from the physical body. Maintaining awareness, they can mentally travel to other locations within this plane of reality, later confirming the accuracy of their observations. They also describe visiting other levels of existence and one of these, supposedly, is the astral plane where those who have died here may be living.

One of these multiplane dwellers is a close friend. I confronted him with the question of whether animals survive physical death. He had told me many times of having contact on the astral plane with persons he had known when they were alive on earth. When I asked him if this was also the case with animals, he answered with no hesitation. "Oh, yes," he said. "I often see animals there, sometimes with other animals, such as several dogs playing or running together, or they may be with a person. It isn't unusual for me to see someone romping with a dog or holding and stroking a cat.''

''But we have no assurance that the animals you observe once lived here?'' I queried.

''Well, I have no way of knowing about many of these animals, of course,'' he responded, ''but I will never forget the occasion when I clearly saw Flip, my old airdale who had died several months before. He was really excited to see me. He wagged his tail and kept jumping against me. I petted him, talked to him for quite a spell, and never doubted the reality of the experience.''

I have helped conduct a number of workshops at the Monroe Institute of Applied Sciences in Faber, Virginia, on expanded states of awareness. These are intense affairs. The sessions are for seven days, starting each morning around six and sometimes lasting past midnight. The experience of the participants vary widely, as can be expected, but there is a great deal of internal scanning, probing beneath the veneer, and becoming acquainted with hidden dimensions of oneself. A great deal of trauma can accrue, but also a new sense of freedom and greater self-identity. New perceptual modes may develop, and as one releases old attachments to the body, out-of-the-body experiences oftentimes occur.

On this particular occasion, a young clinical psychologist from Cincinnati had a very vivid and moving experience of sharing with her deceased mother. It was very real to her and profoundly significant inasmuch as she learned some things about her early life of which she was not previously aware. The physical survival of animals played only an incidental role in this emotional drama and probably would have been overlooked except for a question asked by a member of the group: ''Did your mother seem content with what was happening to her on that plane?''

''Oh, yes,'' the woman responded. ''She was peacefully happy, almost tranquil. She shares with her parents who are there, and one of her sisters, and there are friends. And, then, Penny was close by her side all of the time. She loved that little dog. . . .''

The young woman then resumed her accounting of the sharing between her and her mother and no further mention was made of the dog. Her comments seemed an afterthought, but what was interesting to me was the complete acceptance of the animal's presence. It also is interesting to note that there were several persons in that group who allegedly had experiences on the astral plane and not one expressed surprise that the woman's pet could be on that level.

Fred Kimball has little trouble in accepting the continued existence of animals after their physical deaths. He communicates with them following their death experiences on earth. But then, Kimball has an unusual talent; he talks with animals, as described elsewhere in this book. A worldly man of many trades—merchant marine, Marine Corps coach, judo expert, rifle instructor for the Army, steel processor—Kimball has been involved in psychic research for more than forty years, ever since he found himself carrying on a conversation with a seagull while aboard an oil tanker.

Today Kimball spends most of his time counseling animals and counseling people about their animals. He serves as a kind of interpreter between humans and other members of the animal kingdom. As such, he is in great demand by zoos, breeders, and trainers as well as those involved in research. Quite often he is contacted by someone looking for a lost pet and many times he is able to communicate with the animal and get some bearings on its location.

It was in looking for lost animals that Kimball discovered that communication was not dependent upon the animal being alive. It happened initially when a woman called him at his southern California home and frantically explained that her twelve-year-old Irish setter was missing. Family and friends had searched for three days to no avail. She had heard him describe his work on a local radio talk show. Could he help?

Kimball, during his years as a sailor, had spent a great deal of time in the Orient studying body and mind control. He used these disciplines to attune himself first to the woman, then to other members of the family, the home and its surroundings and, finally, to the lost animal. He saw the large setter move slowly across a meadow and into a wooded area. There by a large tree the dog stretched out on the ground as though to rest. At this point, Kimball explained to the dog that his family was very worried about him, was looking for him, and would it be possible for him to describe where he was. Kimball saw the dog standing strong and proud by a tree. He appeared particularly vital and alert as he stood there for a minute as though listening. While Kimball watched, the setter moved around to another side of the large tree and looked down. There at the animal's feet was his worn-out body stilled by death. Kimball related his perceptions to the pet's owner. She was sure the location was a wooded park area not far from their home where they occasionally had taken the dog on walks. A brief search confirmed their fears and Kimball's observations.

Proof of life after death for inhabitants of this planet other than ourselves? Perhaps not, if we are insisting on hard data. But then, what constitutes hard scientific data? How many witnesses of an event are required for validation? Immortality by its very nature deals with a reality other than the one we are now experiencing. One might even speculate that it would be just as difficult for beings living on another level of reality to prove our existence as it is for us to prove theirs. Any material test we might attempt to apply would be quite obviously inappropriate. So our proof will need to be limited to the testimony of those who have in some manner had contact or communicated with once living beings—animal or human—who in some manner continue to exist.

CHAPTER TEN

Animals in Mourning

Among the extensive evidence that animal psychologist Adrian Kortlandt has uncovered concerning human traits in animals is his witnessing animals in the wild mourning for dead fellows.

One day he left a chimpanzee doll in the paws of a stuffed leopard on a trail frequented by chimpanzees. When the chimpanzees came upon the doll and stuffed animal, they were extremely frightened and highly agitated. After jumping around, running in to get a closer look and then skittering off chattering for more than half an hour, the apes finally abandoned the scene.

That night, Kortlandt removed the stuffed leopard but left the chimpanzee doll at the scene of the crime. In correspondence with author Droscher, the zoologist described what happened the next morning:

"At the first light of dawn the chimpanzee troop returned. In funeral silence they all assembled in a wide circle around the doll. Slowly, a few of them ventured closer. Finally, a mother with a baby clinging to her abdomen stepped forward out of the silent circle. Cautiously, she approached the 'victim' and sniffed at it. Then she turned to the assembled horde and shook her head. Thereafter each ape silently departed. Only one chimpanzee crippled by polio (strangely, these apes also suffer severely from infantile paralysis) remained for a while sitting beside the 'corpse,' looking steadily at it.

It was as though he could not take leave of the face of death.

"Finally he, too, went away. After that there was a sustained silence. All morning long we did not hear a single chimpanzee cry, nor did we later in the day.

"But the high point of my whole expedition had been that chimpanzee female's shaking her head after gazing at the dead body. Of course, we do not know what the animal wished to communicate to the silent onlookers. Perhaps it meant: 'No, unfortunately no sign of life.' But more probably it was: 'No, not any of us.' We are equally ignorant of why that somber mood descended upon all the members of the troop. But an unexpected world always lies hidden behind these chimpanzee faces."

This experience gave Kortlandt an idea. He decided to find out how chimpanzees in the wild would react to a picture of a chimpanzee. He fastened on the jungle trail a zoo poster showing a chimpanzee's head in close-up.

When the first animal saw the picture, it stood still in horror. The rest of the chimpanzees likewise reacted with fear of this photo of one of their own kind. They quickly fled the trail by way of another path. Only the chimpanzee with polio was attracted to the face of death here also. For a very long time he looked silently at the photo, scratching his head.

Kortlandt notes that chimpanzees react with great fright to the sight of dead members of their species and also other dead animals (except those they have killed themselves). A severed chimpanzee arm or leg is sufficient to send a chimpanzee running away in terror. For this reason, the zoologist believes that chimpanzees definitely have an inkling of the meaning of death.

There is likely a connection between this capacity and the chimpanzee's need to rescue members of the horde at risk of his own life. A number of years ago Professor Wolfgang Kohler made some highly interesting observations during a safari.

A chimpanzee was wounded by one of the hunters and was lying on the ground. When it uttered a shrill cry for help, the other members of the horde surrounded it, raised it up, and supported it with "incredibly human gestures, and mouthing gentle sounds urged it to walk." Meanwhile, a powerful ape rushed forward and interposed itself between the hunters and the wounded chimpanzee and helpers. The ape fled to safety only after hearing repeated calls from its companions, indicating that they were safe in the woods.

This behavior perhaps clears up the mystery of why chimpanzees can never be caught in traps. It had always been said that the apes were too intelligent to be caught in traps. However, Dr. Kortlandt found indications that a trapped chimpanzee is always immediately freed by his companions.

And chimpanzees will show kindness and helpfulness to animals other than their own kind. When Kortlandt tied a baby chicken along the jungle path, the chimpanzees freed the small, fragile chick from its bonds. They worked very carefully so not to injure the tiny legs of the small bundle of down. This discovery of affection for other animals strengthened Kortlandt's suspicion that old tales among the African natives might be true—the chimpanzees really did steal human babies.

A human baby could not, of course, be used in such an experiment, but the Dutch scientist decided that he could use a baby monkey as a substitute. He tied a mangabey baby along the chimpanzee trail. When the horde came along, all the chimpanzees gathered curiously around the tiny, screeching monkey. Finally a young and still childless female tried to untie and then bite through the rope—exerting just as much delicacy and care as had been used when freeing the chicken. Unfortunately, the rope was too strong and, after a long time, the project was abandoned.

According to Droscher, wardens in Uganda have for years observed a troop of chimpanzees which included a long-tailed monkey. There could be only one explanation for this mixed company; the monkey must have been picked up by the chimpanzees as a baby, abducted, and raised by them—as a kind of pet.

Other members of the ape family also have an affinity for pets and caring for animals other than their own species. Earlier it was mentioned that a female gorilla by the name of Koko had learned more than six hundred sign language words under the tutorage of psychologist Penny Patterson. On her twelfth birthday, Patterson asked Koko what she wanted for her birthday. Immediately the gorilla drew her fingers across her cheeks, miming a set of whiskers, which was the sign for cat.

Earlier Koko had named two of the household dogs, Apple and Smile, and various visiting cats: Candy, Golden Visitor, Surprise, and Stink, for a cat that had urinated in Patterson's closet.

With the request for the cat, Patterson gave Koko a small concrete statue of a cat. The gorilla kissed and rubbed the object against her cheek. Koko treated the item so gently that when a caretaker brought in three kittens, abandoned by their Manx mother, she immediately was taken by the kittens. "Love that," Koko signed.

She picked up each one of the small kittens and blew gently in its face. After a time, Koko selected a small gray male, rocked it between her legs, and signed, "Koko love soft there," and two days later she named the tailless kitten "All Ball."

For six wonderful months Koko and All Ball played and cared for each other. Koko combed the kitten's hair and when it purred so did the gorilla the best she could in her deep throaty voice. She adorned the kitten with tissue hats and would hold him to her breast, signing, "You mouth nipple."

But when All Ball was seven months old he was run over by a car. Koko received the news of the kitten's death in silence and then, according to reporter Anne Fadiman, she began to hoot the same soft distress cry she made when Patterson had left her as an infant for a night. For two months the gorilla often cried to herself. But when she was asked what she wanted for Christmas,

Koko hesitantly signed, "Cat cat tiger cat." When Patterson brought Koko a yellow striped kitten, she was so excited "she spun around on her knuckles like a break dancer," Patterson reported.

Stories of dolphins caring for humans are legend. Now psychologist David Nathanson relies on six Atlantic bottlenose dolphins at the Dolphin Research Center in Glassy Key, Florida, to help bolster the memory skills and speech of mentally handicapped children. The center is dedicated to "mutually beneficial human-dolphin interaction," and the dolphins swim with, are touched and fondled by, and serve to help teach handicapped children.

Nathanson reports that the children pay closer attention and learn up to ten times faster while working with the dolphins than they do in regular classrooms, where the usual reward is a kiss and a hug from their teachers. The children "prefer a kiss from the dolphins to a kiss from me," Nathanson states. "I'm not insulted by this," he adds. Pictures displaying simple words such as "dog" or "bus" are tossed to the dolphins, which bring them to the kids. If a child pronounces the word correctly, the reward is a swim with the dolphins.

In a recent *Omni* article, "The Day of the Dolphins," by Justin Kaplan, Nathanson recalled that when a six-year-old dangled his legs in the water, a female dolphin named Little Bit, one of the original members of the *Flipper* television series, "zoned in on him and nuzzled him gently. It was striking. The dolphins seemed to sense these kids are handicapped. . . . They perceive these children as a little more helpless than the people they usually swim with, so they're gentler," Nathanson was quoted as saying.

Kaplan explains that a second facility—Dolphins Plus, a private "dolphinarium" at Key Largo, Florida—recently turned over its facility for eight days to Betsy Smith, Ph.D., an associate professor of social work at Florida International University, Miami. She has been working with animal-assisted therapy for fifteen years and wanted to use the dolphin facility to test her theory that autistic children who had not benefited from other types of treatment might become more sociable and communicate better by being with the dolphins.

Ten years ago Smith started studying the responses of neurologically impaired children to dolphins and discovered that those with autism responded quite dramatically. "Dolphins, who have no preconceived expectations, approach others for spontaneous interaction," Smith told Kaplan. While the children's social skills appeared to improve after spending some time with the dolphins, Smith admits that she has not proved that the dolphins, rather than the therapeutic effects of the water, are responsible for her success. Yet she explains that the children who spent time with the dolphins appeared to be more energetic and motivated than a control group that was taken to swim at another beach. Questionnaires and interviews with parents have shown that the dolphin kids demonstrated long-term behavioral and social changes, and she told Kaplan she plans to test the results further with a follow-up study.

Not only have dogs served for many years as eyes for the blind, but dogs are now being used to assist the deaf. They are the "ears" for those who cannot hear. The Hearing-Dog Program is sponsored by the American Humane Society, and the organization uses dogs of all breeds and even mixed breeds. They are recruited by testing the alertness of puppies to balls, mirrors, and various toys.

The January 15, 1989, issue of *Weekly World News* told the story of William and Sharon Cass of Galt, California, and their three children. All of them are deaf but they now "hear" through the ears of Alfie, a young stray mongrel picked up on the streets of San Francisco and taken to the city's SPCA headquarters. Noticing the animal's alertness, a trainer recruited him for the Hearing-Dog Program.

Alfie's training cost twenty-five hundred dollars and lasted for four months. Trainers surrounded the intelligent dog with hamsters, rabbits, and other distractions. They taught him nearly one hundred commands in sign language and how to respond in case of a fire or burglary. He graduated in a class of twenty-five dogs with top honors, and was then assigned to the Cass family without charge.

"Overnight, there was a change in the Cass family," Ralph Dennard of the San Francisco SPCA told the *Weekly World News*. "He became one of them."

The program concentrates on teaching a dog to act in an emergency. "Without this special training we couldn't be sure. After we get through training these dogs, they are very, very reliable. We teach dogs to come by hand clapping, to lie down by pointing the right finger to the floor, to sit by making a sweeping upward gesture from the waist, and to stay by thrusting a palm in the dog's face," Dennard said. He explained that the owners are carefully trained to handle the dogs.

Soon after his arrival at the Cass home, Alfie's expertise was put to use. He alerted the Cass family to possible trouble during a camping trip. All members of the family had gone for a hike in the forest when Alfie came running up. Cass ran back to their camp to discover a stranger leaving. He suspected that it might have been a potential thief who was frightened off by the dog.

Jared Butler, an elementary student in Maryville, Missouri, is assisted by his dog in a different way. Jared suffers from serious bone problems and must wear leg braces to hold his legs in a straight position for standing and moving. His dog, Rio, is with the boy constantly and even tends class with him.

Rio, a black Labrador retriever, helps Jared with keeping his balance. She carries his books and retrieves dropped objects. During the school day, Rio lies quietly at the side of Jared's desk seemingly unaware of the other students. When the bell rings, she jumps up, ready to move at command to the next class. At home, in a household of six other children, Rio gives her entire attention to Jared. The boy has the complete responsibility for the dog. He feeds her twice a day and keeps her brushed and combed.

Jared's mother learned of the program through the editor of the *Weekly Reader*. He put her in contact with Canine Companions for Independence in Santa Rose, California. The organization raises and trains dogs to serve handicapped persons.

According to Ashley Montague, author of more than forty books, human beings can learn a great deal from unselfish animals. The scientist notes that a cat that had a long friendship with a dog suckled the dog's puppies when it died in childbirth. He claims that apes, monkeys, and birds will not allow a member of their species to starve to death.

Montague's position was dramatically strengthened in a recent study by Dr. Jules Masserman, professor meritus of the neurology and psychiatry department at Northwestern University. The Chicago psychiatrist found that a rhesus monkey would willingly refrain from eating because a fellow monkey suffered electric shock when the first monkey ate.

Dr. Masserman placed the monkeys in adjacent cages where they could see each other but were separated by a barrier. One of the monkeys could get food by pulling a chain, but each time it did so, it sent an electrical shock through the other monkey.

"We found the first monkey would starve itself rather than shock the other monkey," Dr. Masserman stated. He added that if an elephant is wounded, the rest of the herd will support him back into the forest where he can recover.

In their book *The Strange World of Animals and Pets*, Vincent and Margaret Gaddis mention several instances where dogs have faced death to save another animal. One of their stories concerns a man named Eldon Bisbee who lived in New York City and owned a small French poodle. One night a taxicab driver came to his door with his injured dog. He told Bisbee that he had been driving through a snowstorm when he stopped to keep from hitting a German shepherd. The dog refused to get out of the way. When he shouted at the animal, it came to his window and whined and then ran to a snowbank. The cabdriver got out of his car and discovered the injured poodle. The shepherd stood above her wagging his tail. After the driver picked up the small dog and put her in his car, he looked around for the shepherd, but the dog had gone.

Dr. W. F. Sturgill was a physician for the Norfolk and Western Railroad. He also owned several fine dogs and was president of the National Foxhunters Association. He treated a friend's dog for an injury suffered on a barbwire. Approximately a year later, Dr. Sturgill heard a scratching on his door. He opened the door to discover his friend's dog, but with him was another dog with injured and bleeding paws. The doctor took care of the injuries and the dogs trotted off together.

Fishing boat captain Lou Lyon of Lantana, Florida, credits a pelican for saving the lives of thirty-six other pelicans. The bird, known as Shakey, was saved from death four years ago by Lyon. Since then, sick and wounded pelicans seek Lyon out and he's convinced it's Shakey's doing. Every time an injured bird seeks help, Shakey can be seen close by.

The Gaddises tell the story of a bighorn sheep, sick and desperate, that came down from the high country and into the town of Baldy, California. She pounded on the door of a physician who nursed her back to health. The sheep then returned to the mountains. But several months later she brought her ailing newborn lamb to the doctor's door.

A pregnant dolphin many times will choose another female dolphin to act as midwife. The baby is born well developed and emerges from its mother's body tail first to reduce its chances of drowning. It is immediately helped to the surface by the mother and midwife. During the infant's first three months, the mother and midwife continually tend the little one, guarding it and allowing it to stray no more than ten feet away. Healthy dolphins often nurse the elderly ones who aren't able to keep up with the rest of the school. Since dolphins must surface to breathe, a sick one unable to get to the surface is nudged and supported by its comrades.

As mentioned earlier in the chapter, many animals will become depressed over the illness of a family member or "friend," and they mourn their dead. When the baby of Washoe—one of the country's top chimpanzee performers in sign language—was ill, the animal pleaded with her keepers, "My baby—I want my baby! Where is my baby?" When she was told that her baby had died, Washoe was deeply dejected and distraught. She finally was able to adopt a baby son but she had a difficult time accepting it at first, according to one of her keepers, Dr. Roger Fouts, who heads the chimpanzee learning program at the Institute for Primate Studies at the University of Oklahoma.

When Bridgette, a gorilla at Ohio's Columbus Zoo, died in October 1987, her mate, four-hundred-eighty-pound Bongo, took over the care and protection of their fourteen-month old infant son, Fossey. According to the gorilla's keeper, Diane Frisch, every night before the two go to bed, Bongo makes a bed of straw for Fossey, then lies down beside him protectively—their bodies always touching.

After Bridgette died, Bongo seemed to know that she had left it up to him to care for Fossey. "Father and son became inseparable," Frisch told reporters. "Bongo shared all of his food with Fossey. In fact, we had to start hand-feeding Bongo because he was letting Fossey eat everything and he wasn't getting enough himself. When he's eating, Fossey leans against his dad. At night they sleep side by side and Bongo always gathers hay that we put in their enclosure to make Fossey a mattress to sleep on. Bongo always preferred to sleep on the floor without hay. But he makes the hay mattress for Fossey because he saw that Bridgette always did.

"When Fossey had a bout with the flu last February, Bongo sat with him constantly, stroking his head and back lovingly. They love to wrestle together and it's amazing to see how gentle Bongo—all four hundred eighty pounds of power—is with Fossey. He tickles him with a big finger under the chin. And when Fossey starts playing with the other gorillas, Bongo is right there to make sure the play doesn't get too rough for his son,'' Frisch explained.

Love for offspring other than her own saved the life of one canine. A shaggy shepherdlike mongrel, who was to become known as Mama Dog, was placed in the Temple, Texas, dog pound with her four newborn puppies by a man who said he couldn't keep her. Animal shelter volunteer Betty Vannoy named the dog Mama Dog because she was such a gentle and loving mother to her litter.

The puppies were soon adopted, but Mama Dog was not so fortunate. After a time, shelter officials considered putting her to sleep but fate apparently intervened. A mother dog was killed by a car, leaving a litter of five puppies. The puppies were given to Mama Dog and she cared for them as though they were her own. With this success, more and more litters were given to Mama Dog to raise. Although the puppies were all adopted, no one offered to take the kind, mothering dog.

But word of Mama Dog's love and devotion spread throughout the town of forty-two thousand and on March 26, 1986, the Temple City Commission named the road to the animal shelter Mama Dog Lane.

Finally, farmers Bertis and Frances Graham came to the shelter and asked to take Mama Dog home. At her new home she has her own doghouse, a freezer full of her own food, and three Bertis granddaughters to play with. In spite of her pampered life, however, the Bertises report that Mama Dog still mothers every animal on the farm, including calves.

Fern and Howard Carlson of Granite Falls, Washington, saved the life of a wounded German shepherd pup and five years later he saved the family from certain death in a house fire.

The Carlsons came home on a cold Christmas Eve to discover a crying and bleeding puppy on their threshold.

He had been shot in the head and left to die in the snow. They rushed him to a veterinarian just in time to save his life. Once he was returned home, the Carlsons decided to keep the puppy until he was completely well and then find him a home. Within a few days, however, they became so attached to the dog they were to call King that they couldn't bear the thought of giving him away. Their children loved the dog, and a grandson rode the good-natured animal like a horse.

The big dog slept in the family's recreation room, and one night King was awakened by a hissing, crackling of fire in the utility room that separated the recreation room from the rest of the house. Instead of fleeing through the open door, King chewed and clawed his way through a heavy wooden door leading to the rest of the house. When the opening was large enough for the dog to get through, he plunged through hot flames and coals to get to the family.

"Can you imagine? We just don't know how he got through those terrible flames," Fern Carlson said. "He's quite a guy."

King ran first to the bedroom where Pearl, the Carlson's five-year-old daughter, slept. "Even when he pawed and whined at her, Pearl didn't know what was happening and tried to shove him away. Finally, he gave up and just dragged her out of bed," Mrs. Carlson stated.

When Pearl realized that flames were engulfing the house, she and King fought their way through the inferno to rouse her parents. Pearl and Fern found a window and climbed outside, thinking that Howard and King were behind them. Then Fern said she heard King barking inside. She managed to get back into the house where she found King standing over Howard who—just out of the hospital following an emphysema attack—had passed out.

When Fern got Howard to his feet, King led them through the black smoke and out the window. "Even if he had died right there, that dog wasn't going to leave until we were all safe," Fern said. "Within a couple of minutes, our bedroom was completely burned. There's no way we could have made it without King.''

The devoted dog's legs and paws were badly burned, his mouth severely torn, and his back badly sliced open during his minutes of heroism.

Two-year-old Margaret Morris of Harvester, Missouri, owes her life to a dirty, hungry dog her father, Bruce Morris, found roaming the streets.

One Saturday afternoon the Morrises left their small daughter and the dog they called Red in a parked car while they shopped across the street. A salesman suddenly said, ''There's smoke pouring from a car across the street,'' and the next instant he shouted, ''My God, there's a girl in that car!''

As Morris raced for the front door he saw Red plunge from a half-open window of the car. ''As soon as Red hit the ground,'' Morris said, the seventy-pound dog ''jumped up, put his paws on the side of the car, and reached his head through the back window and dragged Margaret through the window. Then he pushed her away from the car.'' Flames completely gutted the interior of the car.

Even small kittens have become heroes. He hadn't even been given a name because the family didn't expect to keep him that long. Now he is known as Boots and money can't buy him.

Diane Malcolm found the abandoned kitten and persuaded her sister-in-law, Jane Malcolm of St. Clair, Michigan, to take the animal in. Although she didn't want the kitten, Jane said she would keep it until she could find it a home. A few days later, Jane and her husband Don went out of town, leaving Diane to babysit their two daughters, Holly, one year old, and Jennifer, four.

Both children were asleep in their room, and Diane had fallen asleep on the living-room couch. Around one o'clock in the morning a fire broke out in the basement and the house began filling with smoke, but Diane slept through it until the kitten jumped on Diane's chest and started crying loudly. Diane jumped up, realized what was happening, and managed to get the girls up and outside the house.

"Those people were very lucky," reported Fire Chief Perry Westrick of the St. Clair Volunteer Fire Department. "Smoke was pouring through the house. If they hadn't gotten out when they did, they might never have gotten out."

"When I heard about the fire, I thought that cat saved my children's lives," Jane Malcolm stated. "He's got to be the most special cat in the world."

Eleven-year-old Jimmy Dotson was riding his bike one October afternoon in Columbus, Ohio, while his one-year-old Labrador, Pee-wee, trotted along behind. Suddenly Pee-wee darted from Jimmy's left and knocked the boy off his bicycle and out of the path of a speeding car that approached from the left. Jimmy was safe but the dog lay on the road, his left foreleg mangled by the car. The driver never stopped.

Although Pee-wee had lost a lot of blood, Dr. James W. Harrison, a veterinary surgeon, managed to pull the brave dog through. But the leg could not be saved and had to be amputated. Four days after his return home, however, Pee-wee was once again close by the side of Jimmy wherever the boy went.

One of the heroes of World War II was four-legged, and he received the Distinguished Service Cross "for single-handedly eliminating a dangerous machine-gun nest and causing the surrender of its crew." Chips, part collie and part husky, served with Patton's Seventh Army. When the allies hit Sicily, a number of infantrymen were met by a baptism of fire from a peasant's hut. Before Chips' handler, Pfc. John Roswell, could signal where the fire was coming from, however, Chips broke loose and charged the gun emplacement. After a great deal of noise, four machine-gunners staggered from the hut in front of Chips and surrendered.

Spot, the mascot of Headquarters Company Fire Station in Camden, New Jersey, always slept at the fire station. But on this particular night he chose to sleep across the street in the home of his two young playmates, Nora and Maxwell Souder. That night fire engulfed the home. When Spot could not awaken Mrs. Souder with his frantic barking, he threw his weight against the door, broke it open, pulled the blankets from the sleeping woman. Mrs. Souder got her children to safety but then fell unconscious inside the burning house. Spot stayed with the woman, barking until he finally attracted the attention of a patrolman, and she was saved.

When we give it thought, the events of animals mourning for their own dead and their human companions and creatures risking their lives in the face of great dangers has to say to us that animals deeply care and understand the meaning of love.

In the December 1977 issue of *Human Behavior*, in an article entitled "Far Out," Eleanor Links Hoover stated: "In fact, I would even go so far as to suggest that one of the reasons animals . . . are important to us is their clear superiority in two areas where modern humans have special problems coping—pain and love."

"I have never seen an animal sorry for itself," wrote D. H. Lawrence. And commenting on this statement, Hoover added: "They take their pain cleanly and neatly and accept what they can't do anything about. That's a great object lesson for children. No wonder so many of us adored animals above all else when we were young. But, of course, that wasn't the main reason. The main reason was that they loved us back no matter what we were or did or didn't do. It's called unconditional love and nothing can match it."

I received an interesting letter in which the author discussed the exchange of love and trust between humans and animals. Earl H. Smith, owner of Northland Wolf Colony in Wells, Maine, wrote:

"I've been working with wolves for years now and have found out some very startling things. For instance, if you think, 'I'm going to put that one to sleep,' that 'one' reacts badly, picturing in its mind just what you are honestly thinking. I've found that there are 'avenues' of telepathic communication and any animal may block communication or open up to it at will. An animal has its own demi-frequency, so to speak, and must alter it a bit to receive or send. For humans, it is more difficult since we don't have the automatic control a natural animal does. I've found that each species has its own kind of and level of intellect, suited to its survival, and I term this 'survival intellect,' thus I've begun to find that animals are superior in all survival intellect kinds and levels to human! I can communicate telepathically with a few of my wolves, but others block communication most of the time. What little the wolves have told me indicates that they do not hate or hold malice toward humans, no matter what we do, but they fear and distrust most humans. The rules for rapport with wolves, then, are:

1. Don't try to lie to them, overtly or in thought.
2. Keep a clear, decisive mind at all times; indecision brings distrust, and maybe fear.
3. Be totally loyal to your wolves, or they won't trust your intent. If it is in your mind that [truth] if a criminal tries to break into your facility to injure or kill your wolves, you will use all force necessary to stop him, and even lay down your life for your wolves, your wolves will trust and love you to the very end, and will lay down their lives for you.''

As well as love and trust, animals, as well as humans, can experience anxiety and emotional disturbance. Dr. Michael Fox explains that ''in some ways, animal psychology is as intricate as human psychology, and animals will exhibit symptoms of emotional distress that are comparable to those in humans—separation anxiety, grief, depression, anorexia nervosa, fear, jealousy, even guilt. A dog can mourn a dead master to self-destructive excess, and cats boarded for the summer may become depressed and virtually stop eating. Animals also develop psychosomatic disorders, such as diarrhea, pruritus [itching], and even hysterical paralysis.''

In *The Sixth Sense of Animals*, Maurice Burton tells of an experiment conducted with baby rats. One-third of the babies were kept in one cage, and they were adequately fed and cared for so far as warmth and general hygiene were concerned, but they were never handled by humans. An equal number of rats were treated similarly, but were given mild electric shocks for a number of minutes each day. The third group were under identical conditions, except they were gently handled as often and for as long as the second group were administered their electric shocks.

As the rats grew to maturity, those that were left alone, that is, not handled or shocked, were timid, cowered in corners, urinated frequently, and were unable to endure extremes of temperature or other physical hardship. When they were subjected to the standard laboratory tests for problem solving, they showed themselves to be markedly subnormal.

The second group, surprisingly, showed no effect from the repeated shocks. In fact, they were more or less normal rats, although they did not compare with the third group, which had been handled. These were markedly more friendly than those in the other groups, more healthy, more intelligent, and more able to stand up to rigorous treatment. And they were more resistant to heat and cold, to starvation and to fatigue.

Burton notes that there is a parallel between these experiments and the work of Harry F. Harlow at the University of Wisconsin with artificial mothers for baby monkeys. At the age of two days each baby was given a mechanical "parent" of the same size as its mother with a teat supplying warm milk. One parent was no more than a wire cage. Another was of wood covered in foam rubber with a layer of toweling over that. Both parents had movable heads with reflectors for eyes, and both were slanted backward so that the baby could position itself on the "mother" when feeding.

"Both babies readily went to the artificial mother to suckle, but the one with the wire cage for its mother never went to it when disturbed or frightened, but, like the baby rats that were never handled, tended to cower in a corner and hide its eyes under its arms, even scream when circumstances were not normal or when it was confronted with some terrifying object,'' Burton explained. ''The second baby was far more contented, would spend much time on its cloth-covered parent, hugging it, nestling into it, turning the mother's head round and sitting on its shoulders. When presented with the same terrifying object as the other baby, it would, after brief hesitation, go over and examine it, not run away from it or be terrified by it. The soft touch of the toweling mother somehow gave the baby monkey a sense of comfort and security.''

Interesting how these experiments with animals can be so easily compared with the history of human children who are deprived of attention, nurture, and care!

The need of animals for love and attention prevails regardless of the species. Dolores Robertson's pet doesn't know it is supposed to be a wild animal. She and her father found four baby groundhogs in the country near their Baltimore home. Deciding that the mother was dead, the Robertsons brought the creatures home. They gave three of the baby groundhogs away, but one they kept and named Buzz.

Buzz grew up in the Robertson home and sleeps with Dolores. She explained that she doesn't mind, and on cold nights Buzz nestles close to her and is as warm as a hot water bottle. Buzz likes to eat breakfast cereal and she has her own chair. She doesn't mind if members of the family use the chair, but if a stranger sits in her chair, she immediately tries to push them off.

We can become fascinated by the training programs demonstrating the use of animals to meet some human need and awed by the ability of dolphins and apes to communicate with us in our language. Yet perhaps the greatest lesson we can learn from animals is their unconditional devotion and love. We can learn this lesson, according to Fox, when ''species—plant, animal, and man—cease to be seen as separate entities once the common essence of their being is felt and understood. They are merely different forms of expression—different patterns and frequencies harmonized in the total field of organic interaction of life.''

As Albert Schweitzer put it: ''To think out in every implication the ethic of love for all creation—this is the difficult task which confronts our age.''

CHAPTER ELEVEN

A Bill of Rights for Animals

Every time he saw the cartoon *Ada the Ayrshire*, he would remember the old Jersey cow he used to milk. When the pasture was lean, she would wait patiently at the gate to be let in for her portion of grain that was part of the milking routine. But when the grass was lush and plentiful, he would invariably have to drive the old cow to the barn. And this was never an easy job.

Writing in the *Kansas Farmer* magazine, Oren Long related how his cow would first try to hide. If she failed in this, she would take the path to the barn that led past a pond because she knew he wouldn't follow her into the water. "After a few choice words, and a lot of rock throwing, she would make her next move, which was to run for the trees. There she stood, watching carefully for any mistake in my approach. If I did not stay directly between her and the pond, she was back in the water."

Long recalls that he finally sold the cow and bought one that wasn't so smart; just like he had to sell another cow who learned to open gates; and one that learned to get down on her knees and crawl under fences; and an old ewe that no fence could hold.

"I had a lot of respect for those animals because of their superior intelligence as well as the fact that they were outstanding mothers. But managing a livestock operation becomes impossible with such animals around.

They are much too innovative and other animals soon begin to learn from their example.''

One thing no livestock owner can tolerate is too much intelligence in his domestic animals. It helps to breed animals that are docile and relatively stupid so they will easily conform to the industrialization of animals' production. ''Business comes first—ethics a distant second,'' Long notes.

He writes that while it is becoming increasingly fashionable to discuss animal rights, few of the discussants are willing to answer the basic question: Do animals have rights? Long suggests that the answer is clearly, Yes! ''But only those rights we choose to give them. Does this mean that animals have no inherent rights? Of course they don't. And neither do most human beings. Americans have inherent rights simply because we said so. Then we wrote them into our most basic political documents. Then we passed laws and established institutions to help guarantee such rights. In other words, as humans we have only those 'rights' which we have the power to guarantee for ourselves.

''But it is also self-evident that animals have no power to guarantee rights for themselves. The question then becomes: What rights should we grant to animals? This is, and has always been, an important question. It is important simply because there can be no better measure of a man's character than the rights, or treatment, he gives his animals.''

If we have the power to extend or withhold rights to our own kind and other creatures, how do we determine to whom or to what? Won't our choices—as well as our power to exercise these choices—eventually affect our own rights?

Considering these issues in his book *One Earth, One Mind*, Dr. Michael W. Fox states: ''Many sincere, socially concerned people have asked me why one need bother with animals and with conservation, since they believe that the highest priority is to help mankind. Children before pets, people before animals, human needs before conservation—such priorities reflect a limited world view that lacks a global ethical framework embracing all forms of life, and that fails to see the vital interdependence of all life.

"If we concern ourselves exclusively with man, or with a select few endangered species, choosing some over others, we are making value judgments," Dr. Fox explains. "A transpersonal ethic of reverence for all life makes no such evaluations. If man is more important than other species, then logically we must judge which men are of greater or lesser value than others. The result is an artificial, hierarchical outlook. Reverence for all transcends this ethical bind, which is a flaw in many religions and philosophies today, concerned only with ethical responsibility between man and man and not between man and all creatures. Some see only human suffering as needing to be rectified, but I believe all destruction and suffering are interrelated, since the problems of man affect nature and all life forms."

Psychiatrist Rolla May echoed these sentiments when he stated: "Loss of the relation of nature goes hand in hand with the loss of the sense of one's own self. 'Little we see in nature that is ours,' as a description of many modern people, is a mark of the weakened and impoverished person."

And Dr. Albert Schweitzer noted: "By ethical conduct toward all creatures, we enter into a spiritual relationship with the universe."

Will the growing body of knowledge concerning animal intelligence and behavior and the evidence of the interrelatedness of all life forms provide us with greater respect for other life forms than our own? Will we gain a new kind of reverence for all of life? If we do, in what ways will this affect our lives? Will our new awareness and sensitivity demand different sources of food protein than meat? Will the day of the hunter soon end? Organizations have been formed to protect the seals, the wolves, coyotes, dolphins, whales, certain birds—will this movement grow?

What does the possible extinction of a species mean to us? How might it affect our lives? Scientist Jacques Cousteau has stated that unless we quickly learn to take care of our oceans they will be dead in not too many years. Others have suggested that the demise of life in the seas is soon followed by death on land. Such possibilities are another reason for gaining a greater understanding of animals. Oceanographer John Todd speaks of this need for knowledge. He is quoted by Michael Schofield in an article, "The Smelly Factor," written for *Smithsonian* magazine, as saying: "The oceanographic community has begun to realize the urgency of acquiring knowledge of how marine animals communicate. This is no longer purely an academic or scientific matter. The languages of animals are the means whereby they organize their lives in relation to each other—just as we do. Their communication is crucial to their survival, but the language of fish and other marine creatures probably represents the weakest link in their life histories. Their signals can be jammed or disrupted by extremely low levels of pollutants, and this could have a catastrophic effect on their social behavior. What I am saying is that insidious levels of pollution can alter social behavior in such a way as to prevent there even being a next generation."

Karl-Erik Fichtelius and Sverre Sjolander call for a change in man's attitudes toward the animal kingdom in their closing remarks in their book *Smarther Than Man?*: "Even people who understand the doctrine of evolution intellectually have a hard time feeling strongly enough that man is a part of the living earth. Man needs something to shake him to his roots, to impress him deeply with the fact that he does not own the earth. This something, which might give man the humility he needs, could be a greater knowledge of the other large-brained animals."

The suggestion that man does not own the earth presents us with a somewhat startling perspective. We have for some time believed that if a nation could take and hold a body of land, its citizens could claim ownership.

Once having ownership, we believed—outside of certain restrictions affecting other landowners—we could do anything we wished with the land. It was ours to plow, plant, burn, flood, or place buildings on. Only humans had anything to say about it. No other life form was consulted or given any thought. If animals were involved at all, it was either to work the land or to be a part of the product produced. Now we have to ask if man alone had the right to judge how the earth is to be used. Does my title to the land provide me with greater rights than the animals that live and depend on it? Is man's survival and pleasure the only question of consequence? Are these questions fanciful, or do they have some significance? Do animals have any rights?

Down through the ages, not all human beings were recognized as having rights. Sovereignty has often been limited to royal heads, dictators, etc., who alone determined the extent of rights held by others. Control still remains in the hands of a few in most nations today. The right to vote remained the privilege of adult males until recent years, and not too long ago the males had to be property owners and of a certain race. For centuries, women, slaves, and to some extent children were chattel or property to be disposed of according to the whims of the owner. This is largely the position that animals are in today. Will animal rights ever become an issue? Likely this will depend on what we learn about other creatures than ourselves, what their position—along with ours—is in the universe. A little more than a century ago, a slave-owner would have scoffed if asked if slaves had rights. Is the question regarding animals ridiculous? Will it always remain so?

In his book *Man and Dolphin*, Dr. Lilly wonders what will happen if the dolphin achieves a bilateral conversational level. He suggests that if this should happen, the dolphin will become an ethical, legal, and social problem. "Then," he states, "they will have reached the threshold of humanity, as it were. . . . If they reach the conversational abilities of any normal human being, we are in for trouble. Some groups of humans will then step forward in defense of these animals' lives and stop their use in experimentation: they will insist that we treat them as humans and that we give them medical and legal protection. If the means of their further education in humanity is available, there probably will be an explosive development of such education.''

Some may ask, why this concern for animals when so many humans are oppressed and starving? Any argument that this book has put forth for the respect, appreciation, and protection of animals does not intend in any sense to minimize human problems—and they are many—nor in any manner to distract our attention from high-priority concerns.

But if our considerations of animals were directed only to the welfare of mankind alone, the priority would be reasonably high. This reason is not from the standpoint of balances in nature, nor from the roles animals play in our food production. The issue is greater than these: Our treatment of animals is important to our own internal states. If we are to expand our horizons, to grow, to understand what the new physics means by the relatedness of each and every living thing, then our love and appreciation of all life is essential. In a world where feelings and thoughts are things, our respect and reverence for all living things will be reflected in our own being.

In *Agartha*, Meredith Lady Young states: ''We have come to believe that what makes a human life or another form of life of value is its ability to serve our needs. Within the human community, the moment an individual can no longer perform a task, the entire person is seen as diminished in worth. This belief has a multitude of tributaries. If an individual believes that the value of a person's life is in his ability to do and to perform, then that feeling is apt to carry over to his thought about all life forms, whether they be animal or plant. Further, this individual will tend to believe that the earth is here to serve the human race. A peculiar psychological twist is contained within this thinking pattern. If one believes that all life forms are here to serve him, oftentimes that is translated into the carelessness and privilege of abuse, for it is just another form of the master-slave relationship. If, however, we can become capable of seeing ourselves as equal to all forms of life, we would recognize and know deep within ourselves that what all schools of wisdom and spirituality have taught is true. All is one."

In the last couple of years we have witnessed a mounting public tirade against animal abuse, survival threats to certain species, oftentimes coupled with environmental problems, and the voices for animal rights have grown much louder.

Recently the Humane Society of the United States urged its members to cut up their American Express cards because the credit institution mailed a fur coat catalog announcing: "Fur—Because winter is long and life is short."

"Follow your heart. Drop your American Express," the Washington-based Humane Society told its 830,000 members.

The animal liberation movement is by no means monolithic or even united. Many sympathizers do not agree with some of the direct action taken by radicals resulting in burned buildings, theft of records and research animals, and death threats.

There are large differences about philosophy and tactics. Many, for example, are unprepared to espouse vegetarianism, while others go so far as to feed a meatless diet to their dogs and cats to spare the suffering of a farm animal. It also has closed down some research projects, caused one company to drop its cosmetics line, and improved conditions for some research animals.

Consider the following:

More than two thousand protesters, led by Bob Barker, walked up Manhattan's Fifth Avenue the day after Thanksgiving 1988—Fur-Free Friday. There were smaller demonstrations in sixty-six other American cities.

A research scientist at New York University's prestigious Cornell Medical College made research history when she or the university, or both, yielded to demonstrations and a letter-writing campaign and returned a $530,000 grant to the National Institute of Drug Abuse for a study of barbiturate withdrawal in cats.

In England, a few days before Christmas 1988, the Animal Liberation Front claimed responsibility for firebomb attacks on five of Britain's leading department stores, causing millions of dollars of damage in retaliation for selling fur. Dingles, the largest store in Plymouth, was gutted.

At this writing, police in Norwalk, Connecticut, were holding thirty-three-year-old animal rights activist Fran Stephanie Trutt of Queens, New York, on five-hundred-thousand-dollar bail as she awaited trial on charges of attempted murder and possession of pipebombs. Trutt was arrested on November 11 outside the United States Surgical Corporation, a firm that experiments with dogs and has been a frequent target of demonstrators.

In December 1988, *Bloom County*, a political comic strip, ran a week of satire on testing rabbits for cosmetics.

And in Huntington, Long Island, a tray of vegetarian dog and cat biscuits, Wow-Bow and Wow-Meow, are baked by an entrepreneurial activist.

"At last we're starting to look like a movement, but I think animal rights is in its early stages," explained Ingrid Newkirk, chief strategist and director of People for the Ethical Treatment of Animals (PETA), the most radical of the estimated three thousand to seven thousand groups involved in animal welfare.

A PETA spokeswoman estimates that ten million Americans are involved, and guesses that the operating budgets of the myriad groups come to about fifty million dollars. That's not counting the money held in endowments by the established giants, who tend to be less militant.

The push against wearing fur is the most visible campaign. Ads have appeared atop taxis, on billboards, in subways and buses. Celebrities such as Rue McClanahan and Loretta Swit have participated. Even Princess Di was commended for her refusal to wear fur.

The fur industry tries to keep the activists off the air.

Richard Parsons, executive director of the Fur Retailers Information Council, says furriers have been asked not to give interviews because they tend to "shoot themselves in the foot." Like the time one told a reporter that all American furs are farm-raised. Not true.

"We can't threaten to pull our ads, because that's how we sell our furs," Parsons told reporters. "But we're big advertisers and sometimes we get a pretty good response. Sometimes we can keep them off the air. We try.

"We don't debate them. We don't dignify them. We don't need to defend the use of fur. It's a matter of personal freedom. This is still a capitalistic society, and it is supposed to be a tolerant one."

Sales have not been affected, Parsons says, although the industry is looking to increase the international levy at auction houses to increase its war chest to combat the antifur forces.

"The American fur industry has had locks jammed, arson, bomb threats, and windows smashed," Parsons says. "Giving this movement credibility gives in to more violence."

Dan Mathews, a twenty-four-year-old PETA member in charge of the antifur campaign, says: "The fur industry will be the first domino to fall. We are not asking you to change your life, just give up cruelty."

Besides the furriers, the cosmetic industry, research scientists, and producers of livestock, eggs, chickens, and milk—"factory farmers" as the activists call them—are under attack.

The antivivisectionist faction believes that man has evolved to a point where he can live without any animal products—meat, milk, leather, fur, wool, etc. They feel that neither the cosmetic industry nor medical researchers have the right to experiment on animals; that zoos, rodeos, race tracks, even the household pet is an exploitation of the animal kingdom.

"We are not saying animals have the same rights as man," says George Cave of Trans-Species Unlimited. "Sometimes, we have to make choices. It is easy to choose between a mosquito and a chimpanzee. And if you had a child, a chimpanzee, and yourself in a rowboat and one had to go, the proper choice would be to throw over the chimpanzee."

And what if an animal learns to communicate in human words and can converse about its wants, hopes, fears, thoughts, and sense of self-identity. Can it still be considered "animal" and subjected to captivity and research?

The question is no longer academic and speculative. It has become a moral and practical concern for those involved in successful programs to teach language to chimpanzees, gorillas, and dolphins. And it became a legal question as well when it was recently argued in a Hawaiian court. The precedent-setting court case involved conviction on charges of grand theft against two young men who secretly removed two valuable Atlantic bottlenose dolphins from research tanks in the Kewala Basin Marine Research facility of the University of Hawaii and released them in the ocean.

The dolphins had a right to be free, the men insisted, and this right took precedence over the research on dolphin-human communication on which the National Science Foundation had already invested $350,000. Kea, one of the dolphins, had a vocabulary of twelve words based on sounds and could put together two-word sentences.

The research project aimed to learn more about what goes on in the large, complex dolphin brain, which is about fifteen percent larger than the human brain. Already, it's known that dolphins do better on many tests than chimpanzees and that their memory is at least equal to that of humans.

As explained in earlier chapters, interspecies talk is already well established between human and chimpanzees and other great apes. Using human sign language or computers programmed with symbols, chimpanzees can carry on long conversations with human beings, use parts of speech correctly, and invent new expressions when needed ("finger-bracelet" for ring, "water bird" for duck, "juice fruit" for watermelon).

These chimps can use if-then concepts, persuade humans to supply them with desired new words, manipulate people verbally to carry out their wishes, anticipate future events, joke, play tricks, express feelings, invent swear words, and even lie. One chimp, for example, used 251 different signs for words in a single hour of "talk."

Such experiments make it obvious that at least chimpanzees, gorillas, and dolphins, perhaps whales and other apes, and possibly other species are more intelligent, more "human" in the working of their brains than we have understood. Once we have taught them a means of communicating with us directly by words, how does our relationship with them change? What becomes our responsibility to them?

But it isn't as simple as releasing such animals to total freedom. In teaching chimps and dolphins to become more "human," researchers have also made them less "animal." The two dolphins released off Hawaii died shortly after their release, unable to catch enough fish on their own or the victims of sharks, guesses the head of the research facility.

What to do with research animals who have become so human is a deeply personal and emotional problem, particularly for those involved in teaching them.

Koko, a gorilla with a vocabulary of six hundred words and an I.Q. of 80 to 90, has only been "loaned" from the San Francisco Zoo to Stanford graduate student Francine Patterson, who lives with her and taught her to talk. Ms. Patterson is under pressure to return Koko to the zoo or raise enough money to buy her.

But some lawyers are arguing that as an intelligent, consciously reasoning, communicating being, Koko has individual rights to remain with people she knows and that these are greater than the property rights of the zoo.

"It's ironic that just when humans are beginning to discover the mental abilities of other species they should be threatened with extinction," columnist Joan Beck stated.

"It's increasingly evident that these animals are the most intelligent nonhuman life forms we will ever find in our solar system. Certainly we owe it to ourselves—as well as to them—to learn all we can about communicating with them and to keep this planet a place where they can survive in some new relationship with humans. Mankind needs all the friends it can get."

Oren Long, mentioned earlier, suggests that it is not so much the act of killing animals in itself that offends us so much, for we have been doing that for thousands of years. It is the total lack of any dignity and feeling which characterizes modern animal production "that somehow suggests to some that we have made base and ugly a hitherto respectable practice."

Long points out that chickens used to populate every barnyard. And every old hen used to end up in the stew pot. But no one considered this to be a vulgar or inhumane end for a chicken . . . for every chicken had his or her chance to do its thing before ending up as the star player in a chicken dinner.

Chickens, hogs, cattle, etc., still wind up playing star roles on someone's dinner table, so what is the difference? Long suspects that what some people are beginning to sense about the way domestic animals are raised today is that the practice has gone too far when they are isolated from any type of natural environment. People understand that animals are biological creatures. Therefore, they know that isolating creatures from any contact with the earth and the elements can't be right, that it is an inhumane manner in which to treat another creature, and that all creatures have a right to have their day among the flowers and beneath the stars. And they know that it is a violation of the old hen's "rights" to imprison her in a tiny cage in a dimly lit room, never allowing her to scratch in some manure pile or chase an elusive grass-hopper across the barnyard.

People are becoming more concerned about the current trends toward animal "factory farms," and the manner in which animals are handled in large production units. As the news media and television documentaries have revealed, oftentimes these animals do not have a minimum space in which to lie down, to groom or preen themselves, nor are they allowed to interact with their own kind.

Long explains that the subject of animal rights "concerns not only economics, but is a moral and philosophical question with far-reaching social implications. . . . But one thing is certain now. As one by one the species of wild animals disappear, and as we continue to industrialize the treatment of our domestic animals, the world will become an ever more lonely place for man. For man needs wilderness and the company of non-domesticated animals to maintain his social sanity and his humane qualities."

Somehow these words seem like a century-old echo from the wisdom of Chief Seattle, and one can't help but wonder if we will hear them any more clearly now. He said: "If all the beasts were gone, men would die from loneliness of spirit, for whatever happens to the beast, happens to the man. All things are connected. Whatever befalls the earth, befalls the sons of earth."

CHAPTER TWELVE

The Rise of the Phoenix

His tail wagging with wild excitement, the black mongrel bounded toward the homecoming soldier and excitedly licked his face. Nothing unusual about this typical greeting between a man and his dog after a long separation . . . except for the fact that the dog had been dead for nine months.

The dog, Bobby, had been very fond of the young man who lived next door and they had spent many hours playing and hiking together. Then the man left for the Army and while he was away, Bobby died.

Parapsychological researcher Ian Currie, who tells the story, explains that the man did not know the dog had died and he was delighted upon his return home to have Bobby bound excitedly to him.

"For several minutes, Bobby made a terrific fuss. Then he ran off into a patch of dahlias," Currie explained.

The following day, the young man was told of the dog's death—and that its body had been buried in the dahlia bed.

The man told Currie: "There is no question in my mind that I played with Bobby. I knew him so well there couldn't be any mistake."

This interesting story is by no means an isolated tale. These stories are common to researchers in the field of parapsychology, to animal behaviorists, to writers of animal stories, and to investigators of clinical death experiences and out-of-the-body studies.

Yet, to accept these reports at face value—that animals do survive bodily death—is a thrilling experience for some people but disturbing to others. Anyone who has lost a beloved animal companion can't help but welcome the thought that the animal waits for him or her in some future time and place. However, those who believe in their own immortality but wish to restrict this state to the human species alone, may consider that such inclusiveness diminishes their special favor with God.

Perhaps for those in the latter camp, the words of O-She-Na, an Indian medicine woman, would help: "All forms of life are sacred. Everything that lives is an expression of the Great Spirit. It was created by and has its existence within the Great Spirit," she told me following a meeting at the Indian Center in Wichita, Kansas. "As part of this All That Is anything brought into existence remains in existence, forever—as we understand time— moving toward an understanding of its life force, the Great Spirit."

In *Agartha*, Meredith Lady Young's teacher explains to her how important it is for people to respect all life forms, that failure to do so hinders their own growth. At one point he states: "Since the perfect vibration of life is harmony, each individual life force resonates in a way commensurate with its physical properties (animal, vegetable, or mineral) and its developing spiritual vision. In other words, there are at least two aspects, physical and etheric, to every living force. While Nature is masterful at creating its species in the most beguilingly intricate and yet practical patterns, do not be fooled. All life has purpose and progression both in an ecological and a spiritual sense. Man is too often lulled into accepting nature on its more obvious physical level, failing to respond to nature as an evolving force."

It requires little argument to convince someone who has experienced the return of a deceased pet that animals survive physical death. My own experience with this kind of happening has left little room in my belief system to doubt animal survival. Late one night I was awakened from a deep sleep by the persistent barking of our dachshund, Phagen. I listened for a few moments, hoping he would stop and I wouldn't have to go outside and scold him. The barking continued, sharp and quite insistent, so I pulled on some clothes and made my way to his pen. He was not outside. I looked inside his doghouse with my flashlight, and there he lay. He had been dead for several hours, as the body was frozen stiff. I lay awake for some time, puzzled as to how I could hear Phagen barking so clearly when he had been dead for several hours.

But Phagen was to bark again. For two consecutive nights exactly at the same hour, I heard him barking. Both nights I went outside. The first night I saw nothing but an empty pen and doghouse. But the second night as I approached his pen in the semidarkness of a waning moon, I saw him in the shadows, waiting, and as I drew closer I saw him wag his tail. Awed, bewildered, I reached toward him . . . but in that moment he was gone. He never barked again. Since then, I have asked myself many times if Phagen came back for a final farewell. I might question whether I was experiencing an extremely vivid dream or was having hallucinations. This might be plausible except that my neighbor, who was not aware that Phagan had died, asked me the morning following my final experience if something was wrong with Phagen as he had barked so much on the two previous nights.

In his book, *The Evidence for Life After Death*, Martin Ebon tells the story of a cocker spaniel named Ronnie who died while undergoing an operation. Ronnie's mistress was sitting beside her phone at the home waiting for the operation results. "Suddenly she heard the sound of his dog tags tinkling and his claws clattering across the porch. She held open the door but there was nothing there. She knew her old friend had died and returned home for the last time," Ebon said.

Sages and philosophers down through the ages have

taught that man and other animals are animated by some higher principle than matter and motion, that the soul was immaterial and immortal. The word soul in its original definition stood for the principles which govern life in its various forms. It is true that the modes of explaining it varied. Sometimes it was regarded as the mere harmony of the bodily functions, and some times as a distinct entity of higher ethereal nature, but no essential distinction was drawn between the soul of man and the soul of other animals until a comparatively recent date.

The mental differences between the lower animals and man suggested to ancient philosophers that there should be a line drawn somewhere. To meet the distinction, the Stoics, the disciples of Socrates, maintained that man possessed a rational soul above that of the animal soul which belong in common to man and animals, but nowhere denied the fact of animals having souls.

The Hebrew word for the soul is "nephesh," and the Greek word, "psyche." The two words mean the same thing, and the Greek word "psyche" is the only word in the New Testament which is translated "soul." There is a biblical passage that reads: "To every beast of the earth and to every fowl of the air and to everything that creepeth upon the earth wherein there is a living soul."

Commenting on this passage, Reverend Dr. E. F. Bush states: "The phrase 'living soul' is repeatedly applied to the inferior order of animals. It would seem to mean the same when spoken of man that it does when spoken of beasts, viz, an animated being, a creature possessed of life and sensation, and capable of performing all the physical functions by which life is distinguished, and we find no terms in the Bible to distinguish the intellectual faculties of man from the brute creatures."

Socrates admitted the immortality of all animal life, and maintained that "the bodies of men and beasts are warm and living as long as they breathe, and as soon as the breath leaves the body, not only do warmth and motion cease, but the body begins to decay. Life, therefore, is breath, and breath is air, and as air is eternal and inseparable in its very nature, therefore the soul or portion of air which gave animation to the body will not perish at the dissolution of the body.''

The old school of Platonists claimed that the souls of all living creatures were a part of the universal soul of the world, and that they were depressed or merged in the animal body, and when the body died the soul would go to some other living being.

The hieroglyphic writings and symbolism of the ancient Egyptians seem to indicate a belief in the immortality of animals. A large number of animal mummies were found beside the human mummies. Many animals have special significance in the religious teachings of the Egyptians. The sacred bull, Apis, was kept in Memphis and treated with great reverence. When a person died, he was embalmed and buried in a granite sarcophagus with a suitable inscription carved on a stone. On one, which is a sample of many, are found the following words: ''In the twentieth year, the month Mesori, the twentieth day, under the reign of King Psamethik I, the Majesty of the living Apis departed to heaven.''

The Mahometans advocate the doctrine that there is a Paradise beneath the seventh heaven which is the future abode of the righteous, and that ''there shall be beasts to ride on, ready saddled and bridled and adorned with rich trappings, which will gallop at great speed. Birds shall sing from the branches of the great tuba (tree of happiness).''

Solomon, is one of his despondent moods, ironically asked the question: ''Who knoweth the spirit of a man that goeth upward, and the spirit of a beast that goeth downward to the earth?'' And he noted: ''That which befalleth the sons of men befalleth beasts; as the one dieth so dieth the other; yea, they have all one breath; so that a man hath no preeminence above a beast. All go to one place.''

And Christ was to say: ''O ye of little faith . . . behold the fowls of the air: for they sow not, neither do they reap, nor gather into barns: yet your heavenly Father feedeth them.''

St. John the Divine, who represented himself as speaking through the ''Revelation of Jesus Christ,'' stated that he saw in heaven horses, sheep, leopards, lions, frogs, fowls, and insects; that the beasts consisted of tens of thousands, and that ''every creature which is in heaven and on the earth and under the earth, and such as are in the sea and all that are in them, heard I saying, Blessing and honor and glory and power be unto Him that sitteth upon the throne . . .''

A later Christian, St. Francis de Assisi, noted that ''there is no degradation in the dignity of human nature in claiming kinship with creatures so beautiful, so wonderful, who praise God in the forest even as the angels praise Him in heaven.''

Seventeenth-century theologian John Wesley, founder of the Methodist Church, while speaking of a general restoration of all animal life, stated: ''Nothing can be more plainly expressed. Away with vulgar prejudice and let the plain Word of God takes its place. They [the animals] shall be delivered from the bondage of corruption into glorious liberty, even a measure, according as they are capable, of the liberty of the children of God. A general view of that is given in the eighth chapter of Romans. Then the following blessing shall be given, not only to the children of men, for there is no such restriction in the text, but to every creature according to its capacity: 'God shall wipe away all tears from their eyes, and there shall be no more death, neither sorrow nor crying; neither shall there be any more pain: for the former things are passed away.' What if it should then please the All-Wise and All-Gracious Creator to raise the creatures, which we now call inferior animals, to a higher grade in the scale of creation? What if it should please Him, in the great regeneration, when He makes us 'equal to the angels,' to make them what we are now?''

Closer to our own time, in the last century, Canon Wilberforce, in a speech before the Antivivisection Society in London, said he believed that "these beautiful and useful forms of life, which are sometimes so cruelly tortured, are bound to pass over into another sphere, and that in the great eternal world, men and animals should sink or swim together."

His contemporary, Bishop Stanley Butler, noted: "We cannot argue from the reason of the thing that death is the destruction of living agents. Neither can we find anything in the whole analogy of nature to afford us even the slightest presumption that animals ever lose their living powers; much less, if it were possible, that they lose them by death. The immortality of brutes does not necessarily imply that they are endowed with any latent capacities of a rational or moral nature. The economy of the universe might require that there should be immortal creatures without any capacities of this kind."

And Reverend Joseph Cook was to say nearly a century ago: "Do not facts require us to hold that the immortal part in animals having higher than automatic endowments is external to the nervous mechanism in them as well as in man? What are we to say if we find that straightforwardness may lead us to the conclusion that Agassiz was not unjustifiable when he affirmed, in the name of science, that instinct may be immortal, and when he expressed, in his own name, the ardent hope that it might be so. Shall we, too, not hope that this highest conception of paradise may be the true one? Would it not be a diminution of supreme bliss not to have union with God through these, the most majestic of His works below ourselves?"

The "Agassiz" mentioned by Reverend Cook was Jean Louis Agassiz, a Swiss zoologist and Harvard professor who determined in 1850 the movement of glaciers and that at one time a large part of the northern hemisphere was under glacier ice. As regards the immortality of animals, he stated at one point: "Most of the arguments of philosophy in favor of the immortality of man apply equally to the permanency of the immortal principle in other living beings. May I not add that a future life in which man should be deprived of that great source of enjoyment, and intellectual and moral improvement, which result from the contemplation of the harmonies of an organic world, would involve a lamentable loss; and may we not look to a spiritual concert of the combined worlds and all their inhabitants in the presence of their Creator, as the highest conception of paradise? In some incomprehensible way, God Almighty has created these beings, and I cannot doubt of their immortality any more than I doubt my own.''

Agassiz was supported in this position by Mary Somerville, a member of the philosophical societies and academies of science in England and Germany. On an occasion when she spoke on death, she stated: ''I shall regret the sky, the sea, with all the changes of their beautiful coloring; the earth, with its verdure and flowers: but far more shall I grieve to leave animals who have followed our steps affectionately for years, without knowing for certain their ultimate fate, though I firmly believe that the living principle is never extinguished. I am sincerely happy to find that I am not the only believer in the immortality of the lower animals.''

And in our own time, equipped with laboratories that constantly amaze us with fresh reports on mounting data of animal capabilities and breakthroughs in human-animal communication, scientist and philosopher alike are entertaining the possibility of higher principles in the animal world. Once these higher levels of intelligence and sensitivity are accepted, it is difficult to deny the recipients the same extended states of existence we would hope for ourselves.

The prominent biologist Donald Griffin deals with this question in his book, *The Question of Animal Awareness*. He states that the evidence points to a mental life in animals—that is, cognitive experiences beyond instinct and conditioning. He argues that failure to see this has been a psychological straitjacket that ''may have held back our scientific progress in this important field.''

Commenting on Griffin's words, Eleanor Links Hoover adds in her article, ''Far Out,'' in *Human Behavior* magazine: ''Yea, yea! Maybe someday we will even go so far as to consider the possibility of spirit, or (dare I say the word?) soul, in animals. Why not? What we call 'transpersonal psychology' is doing just that with humans. Lilly has always said that if we could ever conceive the possibility that another species might not only match us, but exceed us in some area, it would do us a lot of good.''

Movie producer and director J. Allen Boone cast his ballot for this in his book, *Kinship With All Life*. Boone's eyes were opened to the animal world when he was asked to keep the great war dog turned movie star, Strongheart. It took him a very short while to decide that he was the student. He explained: ''Strongheart became the 'professor.' I was the 'entire student body,' and wherever we happened to be, either indoors or out, became our 'classroom.' That is how the curriculum functioned as long as Strongheart's physical body was bouncing around in the earth scene. And that is how it still functions. He is still my teacher, and I am still his pupil. Through the illusory mists of time and even death itself, he continues to share with me, through the eternity of goodness, things that are exceedingly important for me to know and to practice.''

Fred Kimball has had a unique relationship with animals for more than forty years. He shares with them in a nonverbal exchange and they tell him about themselves, how they feel about things in their lives, their joys and troubles. It sounds like a modern-day Dr. Doolittle fantasy until one learns that this information checks with what the animal owners either know or can check out. This includes nondiagnosed illness of which the afflicted animal has some knowledge but has been unable to communicate, depression over conditions that once changed brought about relief of the condition, and such things as the animal's knowledge of happenings in the neighborhood that were unknown by the humans involved until they investigated.

For example, a horse told Kimball: "I backed into a rough board in my stable and drove a splinter into my spinal column." The horse was becoming seriously lame in the hindquarters despite the efforts of several excellent veterinarians. When the animal's information was relayed to the doctors, they discovered the patient was correct. The splinter was removed and the horse recovered.

I checked out Kimball on several occasions. He was instrumental in locating lost dogs for two of my friends. I called him and he tuned into the dogs and they were able to pass along a sufficient amount of information that their owners were able to find them. One of the dogs had been locked behind a high-walled yard and could not escape.

My basset Sady told Kimball about our family. Some stories were hilarously funny but accurate. She also told him some things of which I was not aware, including a hiding place for some of her toys. Sadly enough, some time later when Sady did not return home from an early-evening excursion, I called Kimball at his California home. I was to learn then for the first time that Kimball could communicate with animals that had died. He said that Sady had realized she was sick and had tried to get home but she couldn't make it. She had laid down in a meadow about a half mile from home and then her heart completely played out. She told him where her body was located . . . and that is precisely where we found it.

Occasionally people will ask Kimball to contact a pet that has passed on. A representative case was a dog named Lamb. The dog told him that when he passed away he was quite old and suffering from a lame leg. Lamb told Kimball he wanted to die so he wouldn't be a bother to the family. "When I told the surviving family," Kimball said, "they substantiated the dog's story, saying that 'one day, Lamb just lay down and died.' "

Kimball seldom has little trouble communicating with animals, but on one occasion when he tried to talk with a part husky German shepherd named Jack, the dog was so nervous that he wouldn't settle down. The only information that Kimball could pull out of Jack was that he would die in six months. Later this was verified by Jack's owners.

An interesting experience occurred to Kimball several years ago in Silver City, New Mexico, at the St. John's Mine. While waiting for a friend who worked at the mine, Kimball sat down on a cable spool. He soon noticed a large golden-haired dog coming toward him with a great deal of red in the aura about his head, and Kimball recognized this as indicative of an affliction about the head. He patted him and commented, "You must be a good fighter." The dog said that he had been, then he turned and disappeared into a nearby tunnel. A few seconds later, Kimball heard a short bark, and he had a mental picture of the dog tumbling headlong down a shaft, striking his head on something at the bottom and lying still.

Kimball quickly fetched the mine foreman. They found the dog had entered a newly opened section of the mine and had fallen down a forty-five-foot shaft. The foreman explained that the dog was blind (explaining the red aura) and relied on his sense of smell to get around. As this was a new section of the mine, the dog had no way of knowing about the open shaft.

The miners were able to lift the unconscious dog from the shaft and decided that it would be more merciful to shoot him. Kimball, however, was able to tune in mentally with the animal, and he asked, "Are you going to die?" The reply came back: "Not unless you kill me." Kimball told the message to the miners, and their decision was to try to nurse him back to health. In no time at all the dog recovered.

On a recent visit to the mountains, Kimball encountered a mounted deer's head. He had the impression that the deer smiled at him so he concentrated on it. "At first I was saddened that the poor animal had been shot, but then I conjured up a picture of the Donner party which had been lost in the high country. Once I engenerated a rapport with the deer, I learned that the animal had been shot to provide meat for a group of starving people who were living in an old mining tunnel in the Colorado Rockies. The deer indicated that it was not saddened because of the way it had given its life.''

For a number of years I served as a trainer at the Monroe Institute of Applied Sciences. Four or five times each year I traveled from Kansas to the institute's training center near Faber, Virginia, to help conduct workshops in altered states of consciousness. The center was founded by Robert Monroe, a radio engineer and businessman, after he had experienced for more than a decade out-of-the-body experiences. These unusual experiences became such regular affairs that eventually Monroe established an understanding of other planes of reality. Realizing that he could exist and be aware—even acutely so—apart from his physical body, Monroe was able to expand his perceptions and was able to communicate with intelligences other than those confined to a human body on planet Earth.

Monroe's experiences—described in his two books, *Journeys out of the Body* and *Far Journeys*—led him to develop extensive research in the functions of the brain and expanded states of awareness. Training facilities were established at the institute, located on the edge of the Blue Ridge Mountains, and for a number of years, people from all over the world have attended week-long workshops to experience new levels of consciousness.

After spending some time in training at the institute, Monroe asked me to serve as a trainer. Many unforgettable experiences could of themselves fill a book, but they are mentioned here because of a connection with animals. Oftentimes workshop participants will so expand their awareness that they will make contact with friends and relatives who are deceased. While those who have not had this experience may argue in favor of other explanations, oftentimes during these communication sessions, information will be exchanged between the ''living'' and ''deceased'' person in which the living person will learn something they are convinced could not have been gained from any other source.

Upon their return to this plane of consciousness, the workshop participant usually relates—sometimes joyfully and other times tearfully—how wonderful and awesome it was to see and talk with the loved persons again. Of all the things which may be learned during these sessions, not the least is the realization that they are not limited to their physical body and, therefore, death is no longer frightening to them. But what is particularly appropriate here is the contact that the participant occasionally has with pets that have passed over and are existing on the other side.

Having talked with other persons who have attended sessions at the institute, it is not unusual to have persons arrive with the hope that perhaps they, too, will be able to see a loved one again. Seldom, however, do they express the expectation of having contact with a deceased pet. In other words, such contact is most likely not in their thoughts. Yet it happens, and they will talk about the experience excitedly during the "debriefing" meetings.

"It was breathtaking to be with my mother again after all these years," Jack related, "to see her again and for us to share our experiences. When I asked her if she was lonely, she said that, although she missed us, she had many loved ones and friends with whom she shared. Then she added, 'And, of course, Duchess is here with me now.' " Jack explained that his mother's beloved cocker spaniel had died three years after his mother passed away.

"As I passed through a tunnel and emerged into this very bright light, I sensed that I was going to be able to see my brother again. He had died five years before. I felt his presence, and excitement was pounding through me. But quite suddenly, bounding happily toward me, was Racer, my brother's collie that had died shortly after he did. I loved that dog almost as much as my brother did, but I certainly didn't have any thoughts about seeing him again. Yet, there he was, jumping playfully on me and barking, just as he had always done when I had been away for a while. . . . Then he took off and I followed . . . and, yes, there ahead of us was my brother!''

Persons who have had out-of-the-body experiences as a result of clinical death oftentimes will relate how they will view their ill or damaged bodies from a short distance and not infrequently watch while doctors struggle for their physical survival. Sometimes during this interim, while they are apart from their bodies, they will converse with known or unknown entities who are present. A woman, whom I'll call Barbara, told me that during a clinical death experience she found herself walking along a path in a meadow and there, trotting alongside, was her cat Lilly who had died two years before. Suddenly feeling called back to the site of her body, she hurried back along the path, with Lilly running beside her. Then the cat stopped, as though knowing it could not go farther, Barbara said, and sat down in the path as though to wait.

In his book *Unknown But Known*, Arthur Ford relates an experience of pets being with deceased owners. He recalls a nationally televised seance when he was instrumental in putting Bishop James Pike in contact with his son, James, Jr., who had committed suicide. "After the Pike seance, telephone calls were made immediately, to persons as far apart as Los Angeles and London, to check the discarnates' statements," Ford states. "One of the more interesting bits of the 'trivial' variety had to do with two long-deceased pet cats. It suggests something that has long been speculated about in parapsychological lore—that animals as well as humans may survive death.

" 'There's an old gentleman here,' Fetcher said to Pike during the seance, 'who's with your son on the other side. He wants you to check out something that will prove his identity. He has two cats with him that once were pets of his son, who bears the same name he does—Donald MacKinnon. The present MacKinnon now lectures at Cambridge. James, Jr., used to drop in at his lectures.' On the long-distance phone to Cambridge, MacKinnon, who, it turned out, makes a hobby of cats, at once remembered the specific two Fletcher referred to. 'That's extraordinary,' he exclaimed. 'I did have two pet cats— a black one and a gray one—when I was a boy. One disappeared some time before my father's death, the other acted strangely on the day of his funeral.' ''

In many so-called primitive societies is found the belief that, while material expressions of the Universal Spirit change form, all living things have a continuing existence.

Sir James George Frazer, in his classical text *The Golden Bough*, relates the practice of primitive peoples to respect the spiritual nature and continuing existence of animals killed for food. Following are several abbreviated statements from his extensive work:

''Thus among the benefits which the Aino anticipates from the slaughter of the worshipful animals not the least substantial is that of gorging himself on their flesh and blood, both on the present and on many a similar occasion hereafter; and that pleasing prospect again is derived from his firm faith in the spiritual immortality and bodily resurrection of the dead animals. . . . The Lengua Indians of the Gran Chaco love to hunt the ostrich, but when they have killed one of these birds and are bringing home the carcass to the village, they take steps to outwit the resentful ghost of their victim. They think that when the first natural shock of death is passed, the ghost of the ostrich pulls himself together and makes after his body. . . . The Esquimaux about Bering Strait believe that the souls of dead sea-beasts, such as seals, walrus, and whales, remain attached to their bladders, and that by returning the bladders to the sea they can cause the souls to be reincarnated in fresh bodies and so multiply the game which the hunters pursue and kill. . . . The Kwakiutl Indians of British Columbia think that when a salmon is killed its soul returns to the salmon country. Hence, they take care to throw the bones and offal into the sea, in order that the soul may reanimate them at the resurrection of the salmon. . . . In like manner, the Ottawa Indians of Canada, believing that the soul of dead fish passed into other bodies of fish, never burned fish bones, for fear of displeasing the souls of the fish, who would come no more to the nets. . . . With some savages, a special reason for respecting the bones of game, and generally the animals which they eat, is a belief that, if the bones are preserved, they will in course of time be reclothed with flesh, and thus the animal will come to life again. It is, therefore, clearly for the interest of the hunter to leave the bones intact, since to destroy them would be to diminish the future supply of game. Many of the Minnetaree Indians believe that the bones of those bisons which have been slain and divested of flesh rise again clothed with renewed flesh, and quickened with life, and become fat and fit for slaughter the following June. Hence, on the western prairies of America, the skulls of buffaloes may be seen arranged in circles and symmetrical piles, awaiting the resurrection. After feasting on a dog, the Dacotas carefully collect the bones, scrape, wash, and bury them, partly, as it is said, to testify to the dog species that in feasting upon one of their number, no disrespect was meant to the species itself, and partly also from a belief that the bones of the animal will rise and reproduce another. . . . The Lapps expected the resurrection of the slain animal to take place in another world, resembling in this respect the Kamtchatkans, who believed that every creature, down to the smallest fly, would rise from the dead and live underground. On the other hand, the North American Indians looked for the resurrection of the animals in the present world. The habit, observed especially by Mongolian peoples, of stuffing the skin of the sacrificed animal, or stretching it on a framework, points rather to a belief in a resurrection of the latter sort. . . ."

These many years later I still recall the words, as though they were spoken yesterday, of Lois Flying Cloud, my Sioux artist friend of South Dakota. It was early morning and wildlife abounded in the tall prairie grass in which we walked. "All of life forever moves," she said. "If it were to ever stop for even a fragment of an instant, it would cease to exist, for each life form is a spark within the Great Spirit. Its expressions never die or else It, too, dies. . . . Ah, my friend,'' she added, ''time and form are our illusions.''

There is a general metaphysical concept that animals do not have individual souls but that they are part of a group soul. In this model, a horse does not have a separate soul but is a part of the group soul of horse. Following death, the souls of animals are drawn into a reservoir of other animal souls of the same species. When the time comes for new animals of the same species to be born, soul substance is taken from the reservoir, so to speak, into new animal bodies, but no individuality persists. The accumulated experiences of each animal contribute to the pool.

''To assume further that only human beings have 'individuality' and animals have to attain it seems to me to be on a pair with the widespread notion of the white man that 'all Chinese look alike' (matched by the Chinese notion, no doubt, that all white men look alike) and is indicative (I think) of an indiscriminating and imperfect observation of animals who, as any animal lover will tell you, have noticeably unique personalities, even at a very early age. . . .'' Gina Cerminara states in *Many Lives, Many Loves*.

In a thin volume, *The Inner Lives of Minerals, Plants, and Animals*, Manly Palmer Hall states: ''Buddhism is the only major philosophy which has really considered all kingdoms as democratically equal. Buddhism does not recognize any second-class or underprivileged form of life. In its cosmotheistic concepts, Buddhism takes the position that, actually, there are no lower forms of life, unless a child is a lower form of adult. Very few people would justify the attitude that children are exploitable and expendable simply because they are children.''

The support of the position that all creatures realize individual immortality is provided by the Tibetan who states in *The Mahatma Letters*: ''That it is that cardinal tenet which teaches that, as soon as any conscious or sentient being, whether man, deva, or animal dies, a new being is produced and he or it reappears in another birth, on the same or another planet, under conditions of his own antecedent making . . .''

Cerminara points out that ''all life came from the same great Central Source, and all life is traveling, they say, on a long evolutionary pilgrimage back to that Source. Broadly speaking, life evolves from the mineral kingdom to the plant, from the plant to the animal, from the animal to the human, and from the human to the near-divine and then the divine.'' All life forms move through a series of steps from the dense physical, through emotional and mental levels to the near-divine and then the divine. Animal experiences are not in vain, however, and affect the intelligence and capacity of the new outpouring.

Somehow this position troubles me. Immortality devoid of individuality has no meaning beyond the perpetuation of a species. Regardless of how brilliant or stupid a human being is, we are likely to assume that these states have little application as regards his immortality. While we will accept that animals sometimes will demonstrate greater intelligence, sensitivity, awareness, and kindness than at least some human beings, we may deny them immortality simply because they belong to a different species. We do this in spite of arguing that the soul is not constructed of material substance; we seem to believe that the quality of ''soulness'' has something to do with the shape, form, and functions of a physical body.

In the preceding pages we have cited animals of considerable intelligence, intuitiveness, insightful perception, and caring to the point of self-sacrifice for members of the same as well as other species. These qualities were individually expressed and not always in keeping with what we have come to expect of a member of that species. Are these unusual demonstrations expressions of creatures whose consciousness has outgrown that of the species in general? By the same reasoning, how do we compare the mental acuities of Einstein and Leonardo da Vinci with the rest of us? Further, how much individuality are we expressing when we are but a single integral of collective action? Is this something other than herd instinct?

The question then becomes, if we are not willing to assign individual immortality to all life forms even when individuality is clearly there, what criteria would we use to assign immortality to some life forms and not to others? At what point does a creature gain immortality? When it has a grip on human language? Are dolphins withholding the blessing of immortality for us until we master dolphin language?

The man who carries both the distinction and the blame for the development of evolutionary theory, Charles Darwin, had the following to say in *The Descent of Man*: "We have seen that the senses and intuitions, the various emotions and faculties, such as love, memory, attention, curiosity, imitation, reason, etc., of which man boasts, may be found in an incipient or even sometimes in a well-developed condition in the lower animals. . . ."

It would seem that there was no doubt in J. Allen Boone's mind that Strongheart, the great German shepherd, was not only an individual in every sense imaginable but an outstanding one by any measure. In *Kinship with All Life*, he says: "The more I tried to purify my thinking, my character, my purposes, and my actions and to blend the best of men with the best of him in everything we did, the more the big dog and I began moving out beyond the restricting and unreal boundaries of our respective species. We found ourselves operating in the boundless realm of the mental and the spiritual, where each of us could function fully and freely as an individual state of consciousness and together as fellow states of mind in an adventure that seemed to have no frontiers whatsoever."

And how can Essie Nagy question the continuing individual existence of Rexie, her German shepherd? Nagy operated the Gap Tavern on top of cliffs overlooking Sydney, Australia, and the forbidding cliffs drew suicide-prone people. Many people leaped to their deaths before

Nagy obtained the German shepherd. Suddenly the death rate dropped off because if anyone so much as approached the cliff, Rexie would start barking and not quit until help came. Not infrequently Rexie would grab Nagy's dress and pull her outside if someone was on the cliffs.

One day Rexie died and yet the barking did not stop. Nagy hears the dog and sometimes feels him pulling on her skirt. Every time this has happened, she has found someone about to take a leap from the cliffs. Attorney Clifford Gordon told Australian reporters: "Everybody around here knows the dog was responsible for saving dozens of lives. Until she took to patroling the cliff top, the place was notorious for suicides, Rexie largely stopped all that—and now Mrs. Nagy is doing the same. It's absolutely mystifying the way she knows somebody is about to jump. I don't doubt at all that it's the spirit of the dead dog which warns her."

Terry Comfort of Lawrence, Kansas, doesn't doubt that one of her cats was still around for nine months after its death. Terry and her family had the large Chinchilla Persian for sixteen years. He slept in the crib of Terry and Kent's daughter, Colby, and they remained close. Morning was his talkative time, Terry explained, particularly when family members were trying to get ready in the bathroom. He didn't change this pattern after he died, for both Terry and Colby would be aware of his presence and hear his voice.

In answer to the questions, Do animals have consciousness after death and what is the difference between the Spirit of an animal and that of man, Manly Palmer Hall states in *Questions and Answers*: "Philosophy teaches us that the Eternal Essence, which we call God, and which is the sum and origin of all things, is as much in the animal as it is in man, and therefore the plant of the field or the animals that roam among the hills is as surely an immortal creature as is man. The difference between the various forms of life which we see is not in the Invisible Spiritual nature which is within, but is rather a difference of unfoldment of the objective vehicles by means of which the invisible nature manifests itself.

"As the animal has not the rational faculties of man, man's sphere of consciousness after death would be inconceivable to creatures with plant or animal consciousness. But the Law of Evolution is gradually unfolding the potentialities of the lower kingdoms of nature and in time the animals will unfold its consciousness to a degree fully as great as that of man, and all together the mineral, the plant, the animal, and the man are being swept along to endless stages of growth and unfoldment, until finally all attain that perfection which is the ultimate condition of unity with Eternal Life.

"Because the superphysical bodies are not highly individualized, there is little after-death consciousness. The animal soul or entity returns almost immediately to the physical world. The interval between incarnations is frequently only a few weeks, whereas man, who has more highly individualized his subjective nature, usually remains out of incarnation for at least one thousand years."

Cerminara sums up the matter rather well: "It would hardly seem likely that only one class of life, the human, is making purposive advances upward, and all other classes of life are merely static props to the human drama. All other classes of life do seem to participate in a dynamic evolutionary process, and there are a number of structural and biological similarities between the various kingdoms. It is far more logical, therefore, to infer that there is one far-off divine event, as Tennyson put it, toward which the whole creation moves."

CHAPTER THIRTEEN

The Implications

When Christopher Columbus returned to Europe after his first Atlantic Ocean cruise, he found it more than a little difficult to convince some of the homefolk that he had actually sailed to the other side of that awesome body of water. And even more unbelievable were his stories of finding human beings living there, for surely there couldn't possibly be people on some other side.

It is easy for us today to laugh at the provincialism of the fifteenth-century European. Our universe has grown considerably since Columbus's day. We cross that same ocean in a matter of hours and our spaceships probe the outer reaches of the solar system. But despite our cosmic sophistication, we are still somewhat provincial. It is not so difficult to imagine historians looking back a couple of centuries from now and becoming amused over our beliefs that we were the only really intelligent creatures in the universe. Perhaps somewhere in future time there will be beings on the earth who flatly deny that they descended from homo sapiens. Yet most of us today are disbelieving of reports of extraterrestials landing on earth. We dismiss these stories as the products of someone's imagination. "No," we are likely to say, "there's no truth to these tales."

We have been so indoctrinated with the ideology of our unique status in the universe that it has been nearly impossible for us to entertain thoughts of intelligent life on other planets. Extraterrestials are not part of our consciousness. Even though we may deal with them in science fiction and are entertained by movies and television shows about them, ET's do not exist in our belief systems.

We remain equally provincial when it comes to accepting intelligence in other earth dwellers than ourselves. We are the intelligent inhabitants of this planet, and that's that. We grew up on stories and cartoons of cute animals behaving like people but were informed as we grew older that it was important to separate fantasy from reality. It should be obvious to us, we were told, that animals are on the earth to serve mankind by way of food, clothing, work, protection, pets for our amusement, or to serve our curiosity. That animals might have thoughts, hopes, anxieties, fears, and designs of their own have not fit into our view of life. This was not part of our consciousness.

Somewhat as a number of the leading scientists of the day refused to look into the early microscopes because they knew they wouldn't see anything, and if they did they wouldn't believe it, we have been blind to a world all around us because, if we were the most intelligent creatures on the globe, how could we possibly learn from creatures lower than us?

But we may not be able to protect our belief system very much longer from the intrusion of equal or greater intelligences from outer space. And in our immediate presence are creatures—despite their fur, hooves, beaks, fins, and claws—we may have to accept as something more than useful props in our environment. What would happen if we came to realize that animals have a great deal more intelligence, feelings, thoughts, etc., than we have been giving them credit for? What if we were to learn that other earth creatures could provide us information we didn't already possess, and a knowledge that could be useful in our lives? What if, while we are teaching them our language, they would find a way to teach us theirs, and as a result of this communication breakthrough we would realize that in some ways these other creatures were equal or superior to ourselves?

It is not so difficult to imagine spaceships landing on earth and their crews, finding us very primitive in comparison to themselves, saying to one another, "Well, it's not as though they feel or have any real intelligence. . . ." To them, we would be considered second-class citizens and they might easily decide that it was foolish to extend to us any meaningful rights. Perhaps this scenario is farfetched, and yet that is exactly how we have treated every other living entity on this planet.

How will we handle the new and growing information on animal intelligence? Will this knowledge force us to reevaluate our interspecies relationships? Will our consciences allow us to continue to withhold all rights and will we hold ourselves responsible for their deaths by our hands? Will we no longer be willing to slaughter them for food? Work and treat them as we see fit? Will the human race be better or worse off because of these insights? And what if we were to learn that all life forms are progressing toward a spiritual awakening, that animals, as we, pass in and out of material form over the course of a long history in the pursuit of some divine perfection?

"Perhaps it's time to think about a Magna Carta for animals, granting them human rights depending on their level of intelligence," Carl Sagan has stated.

Manly Palmer Hall points out that we have taken the position that man is unique and a superior creature, and that the universe was largely made for his support and comfort. He suggests, however, that this idea is beginning to fade and that we are looking around for a more reasonable explanation of life.

In *The Inner Lives of Minerals, Plants, and Animals*, Hall offers readers a brief history of the development of man's attitudes toward animals. He explains that writings associating different animals with various moral virtues relating to human behavior originated in Egypt before the Christian era. These works were written at a time when zoology was a branch of theology. "These collections of pious reflections were called bestiaries and contributed to the art of physiognomy according to which persons resembling certain animals also portrayed some of their characteristics. Although favorite reading for centuries, bestiaries were among the intellectual casualties resulting from the rise of physical sciences."

With the dawn of science, Hall notes that our relating the nature and qualities of character and conscience to animals became eroded. "Science regarded the other kingdoms of nature as expendable, anything that tended to advance the cause of man was legitimate no matter how much it plundered the natural resources of the earth. Industry followed this general point of view, and as a result of this trend, we find ourselves in the presence of a number of commodity shortages which are giving concern. . . ."

Perhaps we have underestimated the intelligence of animals because we have imagined that our concepts of achievement are the only ones, that the development of technology and the establishment of a complex civilization are the only indicators of growth. We have decided that the only intelligence is our kind. Since we assumed that the so-called lower creatures had nothing to teach us, we have not listened. Because of our myopia and inadequacies, we have lived in the world, but a great deal of it has passed us by.

The secret of listening was discussed by Boone in *Kindship with all Life*. He mentioned that some people endeavor to establish communication with animals but fail to build the bridges for two-way traffic. "Their bridges permitted thought traffic to flow from them to their dogs, but not from their dogs to them. They were eager senders but not eager receivers. And that automatically threw any real correspondence out of balance."

Boone spoke of his experiences in learning to truly communicate with Strongheart: "In trying to hear and understand Stongheart when he silently spoke to me, or rather when he was spoken through by the Mind of the

Universe, my conventional ears were great handicaps. They were geared to harsh and discordant earth sounds and were unable to pick up the delicate universal mental language, especially as it came through a dog. I made real progress only when I gave the most diligent heed to the 'practically lost art of listening,' which, as William Yeats maintained, 'is the nearest of all arts to Eternity.' ''

One early evening, on a hike through a meadow with Baron, my German shepherd, he suddenly stopped and sat down in front of me. I tried to move past him, but he placed himself in front of me again and I realized he was trying to tell me something. He kept looking at me until I, too, sat down in the grass, and then he turned away from me and gazed at the setting sun. His eyes fixed to the west, he sat immobile until awhile after the sun had set. When he came out of his reverie, he nudged me and we took off again across the meadow, he playfully, myself in awe.

''For all these living entities, like man, possess not only an outer physical form but an inner spiritual component. Indians must kill a deer or fell a pine in order to utilize its physical form for their material needs. But before doing so, they invoke its spiritual life as a source of psychic energy also. Such rituals were conducted throughout all America and ancient Mexico, and they are still observed today in the Southwest. As I see it, we must graduate to this belief, to attune ourselves to both the inner and the outer realities of life if we are to close the widening rupture between our minds and our hearts. By rupture, I mean this: In ruthlessly destroying nature, man, who is also part of nature, ruptures his own inner self. For man's unconscious is equated to and rooted in nature. And by our destructive and materialistic rationalism, we have alienated our conscious self from the earthy substratum of our essential being. . . . We've got to listen to the voice of the secret and invisible spirit of the land itself.''

When I discovered this passage, I read it several times.

It made me remember the words of Lois Flying Cloud spoken to me many years ago: "If you will learn to listen to the wind when it calls," she said, "and discover the language of other animals than ourselves, you will never lose the center of yourself."

The passage quoted above was from an interview that James Peterson conducted with Frank Waters. It was published in the May 1973 issue of *Psychology Today* and was entitled "Lessons from the Indian Soul." Frank Waters, author of *The Colorado Book of the Hopi* and *The Man Who Killed the Deer*, is considered one of today's foremost writers on the American Indian. What is so appealing about Waters's writing is that one is told that language can be a great deal more than a rosary of words, that the deepest, most profound communication comes from the heart and not the mind.

What was so hauntingly beautiful about *Jonathan Livingston Seagull* was not that the book was a modern mythology presenting hidden truths in an allegorical fashion. Certainly it was this, but while one understood that the story pertained to man's sojourn upon this and other worlds, the reader was almost equally sure that the story was also about seagulls. He would tell himself that it was not, committed as we are to the Judeo-Christian belief that immortality is reserved for our own species. But something within our unconscious domains, or at the intuitive levels of our hearts, tells us we share our destiny with the great white bird. The delight and optimism we experienced in reading the words, which Bach himself claimed came to him from another dimension, defied any logical convictions to the contrary, and we found ourselves basking at least for the moment in a certain knowledge that all of life is one.

Job tells us: "But ask now the beasts, and they shall teach thee; and the fowls of the air, and they shall tell thee . . ." We have a tendency to equate communication with words; even assigning descriptive phrases to music and art, forgetting that they are languages in themselves. If one is to comment accurately on music, he must do so with music, and to a painting he must respond with a painting. Words have made us forget our beginnings. We have used them to chronicle our experiences through the ages. They have been the building blocks of civilization. But they have taken us away from ourselves, and we have imagined that to label something is to understand it. Words have been our passport out of Eden, but they have served to alienate us from the other inhabitants of this planet. Perhaps we imagined they had nothing to offer us . . . except their flesh, their labor, their loyalty and devotion. Apparently we were wrong. We may even discover we are not the wisest dwellers in the kingdom. In any case, we are beginning to listen to other voices in the wind.

"Even people who understand the doctrine of evolution intellectually have a hard time feeling strongly enough that man is a part of the living earth. Man needs something to shake him to his roots, to impress him deeply with the fact that he does not own the earth. This something, which might give man the humility he needs, could be a greater knowledge of the other large-brained animals," Karl-Erik Fichtelius and Sverre Sjolander tells us in *Smarter Than Man?*

Perhaps we should remember a prayer first uttered by St. Basil, Bishop of Caesarea, in A.D. 370:

"O God, enlarge within us the sense of fellowship with all living things, our little brothers to whom Thou has given this earth as their home in common with us. May we realize that they live not for us alone, but for themselves and for Thee, and that they love the sweetness of life even as we, and serve Thee better in their place than we in ours."

In our egocentric lives we have come to believe that what makes a human life and other living things of value are their ability to serve our needs. This individual, Meredith Lady Young tells us in *Agartha*, "will tend to believe that the earth is here to serve the human race. A peculiar psychological twist is contained within this thinking pattern. If one believes that all life forms are here to serve him, oftentimes this is translated into carelessness and privilege of abuse, for it is just another form of the master-slave relationship. If, however, we can become capable of seeing ourselves as equal to all forms of life, we would recognize and know deep within ourselves that what all schools of wisdom and spirituality have taught us is true. All is one.''

And Young's teacher tells her: ''It becomes increasingly important for Earth's people to seriously consider the notion of intelligent nonhuman life on planet Earth as more than poetry. The right to live with mutual consideration and respect needs to be the newly forged path of an aware society. Men and women cannot respond appropriately and lovingly if they lack an education in planetary awareness, yet this lack of knowledge can no longer exist as the excuse for Earth's rampant destruction and lack of consideration for other living forces. . . .''

Vincent and Margaret Gaddis note in *The Strange World of Animals and Pets* that ''. . . each human being, animal, and plant is related to all other life. . . . All of us who live are a part of the universal whole, fellow creatures in the cosmos, responding to the ceaseless ebb and flow of the universe. And there are other voices from out of the deep that speak in languages still unknown to man.''

In our search for the basic substratum of the universe, as particle theory gives way to wave theory and we seek for a unified field theory that will tie it all together, perhaps the bottom line is that all is consciousness . . . maybe then the world will have become a thought.

''We become enchanted with the form of the horse or of the owl and imagine that they are limited in their intelligence and being and forget that they are only expressions of the All Knowing. Would we limit It?'' Lois Flying Cloud asked. ''If this small creature is the Great Spirit expressing Himself, why do we not listen? Why do we imagine that God would create all manner of living things out of the substance of His being and yet limit Himself to existing within the human? How could He manage that? How could the All Knowing care for the hawk when He created him and care for him soaring in the sky, but not care when his body lies no longer moving on the ground? Why would He do that?'' And later she added: "Mysteries? Yes, there will always be these, but there would be fewer if we were to find that all of these creatures exist within and not outside of us.''

Hall asks us to consider that it is not consciousness which grows "but the body through which this consciousness manifests. From a physical standpoint it seems that life is unfolding, but in reality life is ideating by overcoming the limitations of the form which it occupies. . . . Evolution makes possible the production of vehicles suitable to the needs of the being that inhabits them. . . . All things reveal life because life is in them, and all things move toward the fulfillment of their own eternity because eternity is in them. . . .''

Hall asks: "Can God destroy that which He has created? Is life expendable or is it eternal? To those who assume that life, consciousness, and reality are all synonymous terms, there can be no death without compromising the existence of God. Many philosophically minded people have come to the conclusion that there is no death. If this is true, it applies not only to man but to any creature that is capable of being destroyed physically. For if life is one, eternal, and inevitable, then physical destruction can only occur on a level of phenomena . . .''

And what of an animal that lays down its life for its human master? Gary Zuhav asks in *The Seat of the Soul*. "This is as legitimate a sacrifice of love of life as it is for a human, because in that instance the animal realizes that it is willingly releasing its life. That, for an animal, is graduation to the human experience, or to its next higher level.''

That animals, too, are on a journey, moving through and beyond the form in which we find them, is an idea echoed by Cerminara in *Many Lives, Many Loves*. She states: "Animals are related to us much more closely than we think. Though they lack speech, their mental processes are not very unlike our own. They are similar to us in their fears, their pains, their affections, their frustrations, their terrors, their devotions, their gratitudes, in short, in all their emotions, even though they may know them in lesser complexity and degree than we. They are, as Mohammed said, a people like ourselves. Regarded from the evolutionist and reincarnationist point of view, they must be a people struggling along like ourselves, on the long, difficult road to perfection."

There is an old Moor verse that goes:

> "We may enjoy in realms above
> The blessings of eternal love:
> When man, released from pain and care,
> With bird and beast shall heaven share."

BIBLIOGRAPHY

Boone, J. A. *Kinship with all Life*. New York: Harper & Brothers, 1952.

Brown, B. *ESP with Plants and Animals*. New York: Essandess Special Editions, 1971.

Burton, M. *The Sixth Sense of Animals*. New York: Taplinger, 1973.

Castaneda, C. *The Teachings of Don Juan: A Yaqui Way of Knowledge*. New York: Ballantine Books, Inc., 1969.

Cerminara, G. *Many Lives, Many Loves*. William Sloane Associates, 1963.

Cowley, G. "The Wisdom of Animals," *Newsweek*, May 23, 1988.

Dorst, J. *The Migration of Birds*. Quoted in Copley News Service Feature, June 2, 1968.

Droscher, V. *The Friendly Beast*. New York: E. P. Dutton & Co., Inc., 1971.

Dunlap, J. *Exploring Inner Space*. New York: Harcourt, Brace and World, 1971.

Eckstein, G. *Everyday Miracle*. New York: Harper & Brothers, 1940.

Emlen, J. T. and Penny, R. L. *Scientific American*, October 1966.

Fadiman, A. "The Gorilla Who's Smitten With Kittens," *Life*, July 1985.

Fichtelius, K. E. and Sjolander, S. *Smarter Than Man?* New York: Ballantine Books, 1974.

Fodor, N. *Between Two Worlds*. West Nyack, New York: Parker Publishing Co., 1964.

Ford, A. *Unknown But Known*. New York: Harper & Row, 1968.

Fox, M. W. "Animals Can't Think? Think Again," *McCall's*, March 1984.

Frazer, J. *The Golden Bough*. New York: The Macmillan Company, 1969.

Gaddis, V. and M. *The Strange World of Animals and Pets*. New York: Cowles Publishing Company, Inc., 1970.

Hall, M. *The Inner Lives of Minerals, Plants, and Animals*. Los Angeles: Philosophical Research Society, Inc., 1973.

Heindel, M. *The Rosicrucian Cosmo-Conception*. Oceanside, California: Rosicrucian Fellowship, 1911.

Hix, E. *Strange as it Seems*. New York: Doubleday & Co., 1953.

Hoover, E. L. "Far Out," *Human Behavior*, December 1977.

Lilly, J. *Man and Dolphin*. Garden City, N.Y.: Doubleday & Co., 1961.

Kaplan, J. "The Day Of the Dolphins," *Omni*, August 1988.

Long, O. "Do Animals Have Rights?" *Kansas Farmer*, August 15, 1981.

Lorenze, K. *King Solomon's Ring*. New York: Time Inc., 1962.

Michell, J. *The View Over Atlantis*. New York: Ballantine Books, 1969.

Monroe, R. *Journeys Out of the Body*. New York: Doubleday, 1973.

Morris, R. L. "Animals and ESP," *Psychic*, October 1973.

Mouras, B. P. "Buckle Your Seat Belts, It's Going to be a Bumpy Night," *Mainstream*, Spring 1986.

Neihardt, J. *Black Elk Speaks*. New York: Pocket Books, 1972.

Ocean, J. "Dolphin Connection," *Challenge*, Summer 1989.

Packard, V. *Animal I.Q.* New York: Dial Press, 1950.

Palmer, J. D. *Natural History*, March 1966.

Papashvily, G. and H. *Dogs and People*. Philadelphia: J. B. Lippincott and Co., 1954.

Pierakos, J. "The Energy Field in Man and Nature," Institute of Bioenergetics Analysis, n.d.

Roark, E. *Just a Mutt*. New York: Whittlesey House, 1947.

Rucks, L. *Oklahoman* and *Times*, April 24, 1976.

Simmons, J. D. "The Great Whales," *TV Guide*, February 11, 1978.

Storer, D. *Amazing But True Animals*. Greenwich, Connecticut: Fawcett Publications, 1976.

Stromberg, G. *Man, Mind, and the Universe*. Los Angeles: Science of Mind, 1973.

Sziland, L. *The Voice of the Dolphin and Other Stories*. New York: Simon & Schuster, 1961.

Waite, D. V. "Do Animals Really Possess A Sixth Sense?" *Probe The Unknown*, May 1975.

Watson, L. *The Romeo Error*. Garden City, N.Y.: Anchor Press/Doubleday, 1974.

———, *Supernature*. New York: Doubleday, 1973.

Young, M. *Agartha*. Warpole, N.H.: Stillpoint Publishing, 1984.

Zukav, G. *The Seat of the Soul*. New York: Simon & Schuster, 1989.

About the Author

Bill D. Schul has been a newspaper reporter, editor, and social scientist. He is the bestselling author of *The Psychic Frontiers of Medicine* and *The Psychic Power of Animals*, and coauthor of *The Secret Power of Pyramids* and *The Psychic Power of Pyramids*.